S0-AZV-759

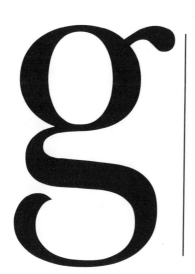

WORD TRANSLATIONS

Math Strategy Guide

This comprehensive guide analyzes the GMAT's complex
word problems and provides structured frameworks for
attacking each question type. Master the art of translating
challenging word problems into organized data.

Word Translations GMAT Strategy Guide, Third Edition

10-digit International Standard Book Number: 0-9818533-7-4
13-digit International Standard Book Number: 978-0-9818533-7-6

Copyright © 2008 MG Prep, Inc.

ALL RIGHTS RESERVED. No part of this work may be reproduced or used in any form or by any means—graphic, electronic, or mechanical, including photocopying, recording, taping, Web distribution—without the prior written permission of the publisher, MG Prep Inc.

Note: *GMAT, Graduate Management Admission Test, Graduate Management Admission Council,* and *GMAC* are all registered trademarks of the Graduate Management Admission Council which neither sponsors nor is affiliated in any way with this product.

8 GUIDE INSTRUCTIONAL SERIES

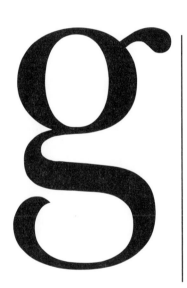

Math GMAT Strategy Guides

Number Properties (ISBN: 978-0-9818533-4-5)

Fractions, Decimals, & Percents (ISBN: 978-0-9818533-2-1)

Equations, Inequalities, & VICs (ISBN: 978-0-9818533-1-4)

Word Translations (ISBN: 978-0-9818533-7-6)

Geometry (ISBN: 978-0-9818533-3-8)

Verbal GMAT Strategy Guides

Critical Reasoning (ISBN: 978-0-9818533-0-7)

Reading Comprehension (ISBN: 978-0-9818533-5-2)

Sentence Correction (ISBN: 978-0-9818533-6-9)

*Manhattan*GMAT
the new standard

September 30th, 2008

Dear Student,

Thank you for picking up one of the Manhattan GMAT Strategy Guides—we hope that it refreshes your memory of the junior-high math that you haven't used in years. Maybe it will even teach you a new thing or two.

As with most accomplishments, there were many people involved in the various iterations of the book that you're holding. First and foremost is Zeke Vanderhoek, the founder of Manhattan GMAT. Zeke was a lone tutor in New York when he started the Company in 2000. Now, eight years later, MGMAT has Instructors and offices nationwide, and the Company contributes to the studies and successes of thousands of students each year.

These 3rd Edition Strategy Guides have been refashioned and honed based upon the continuing experiences of our Instructors and our students. We owe much of these latest editions to the insight provided by our students. On the Company side, we are indebted to many of our Instructors, including but not limited to Josh Braslow, Dan Gonzalez, Mike Kim, Stacey Koprince, Jadran Lee, Ron Purewal, Tate Shafer, Emily Sledge, and of course Chris Ryan, the Company's Lead Instructor and Director of Curriculum Development.

At Manhattan GMAT, we continually aspire to provide the best Instructors and resources possible. We hope that you'll find our dedication manifest in this book. If you have any comments or questions, please e-mail me at andrew.yang@manhattangmat.com. I'll be sure that your comments reach Chris and the rest of the team—and I'll read them too.

Best of luck in preparing for the GMAT!

Sincerely,

Andrew Yang
Chief Executive Officer
Manhattan GMAT

HOW TO ACCESS YOUR ONLINE RESOURCES

Please read this entire page of information, all the way down to the bottom of the page! This page describes WHAT online resources are included with the purchase of this book and HOW to access these resources.

If you are a registered Manhattan GMAT student and have received this book as part of your course materials, you have AUTOMATIC access to ALL of our online resources. This includes all practice exams, question banks, and online updates to this book. To access these resources, follow the instructions in the Welcome Guide provided to you at the start of your program. Do NOT follow the instructions below.

If you have purchased this book, your purchase includes 1 YEAR OF ONLINE ACCESS to the following:

> **6 Computer Adaptive Online Practice Exams**
>
> **Bonus Online Question Bank for *WORD TRANSLATIONS***
>
> **Online Updates to the Content in this Book**

The 6 full-length computer adaptive practice exams included with the purchase of this book are delivered online using Manhattan GMAT's proprietary computer-adaptive test engine. The exams adapt to your ability level by drawing from a bank of more than 1,200 unique questions of varying difficulty levels written by Manhattan GMAT's expert instructors, all of whom have scored in the 99th percentile on the Official GMAT. At the end of each exam you will receive a score, an analysis of your results, and the opportunity to review detailed explanations for each question. You may choose to take the exams timed or untimed.

The Bonus Online Question Bank for *WORD TRANSLATIONS* consists of 25 extra practice questions (with detailed explanations) that test the variety of Word Translation concepts and skills covered in this book. These questions provide you with extra practice *beyond* the problem sets contained in this book. You may use our online timer to practice your pacing by setting time limits for each question in the bank.

The content presented in this book is updated periodically to ensure that it reflects the GMAT's most current trends. You may view all updates, including any known errors or changes, upon registering for online access.

Important Note: The 6 computer adaptive online exams included with the purchase of this book are the SAME exams that you receive upon purchasing ANY book in Manhattan GMAT's 8 Book Strategy Series. On the other hand, the Bonus Online Question Bank for *WORD TRANSLATIONS* is a unique resource that you receive ONLY with the purchase of this specific title.

To access the online resources listed above, you will need this book in front of you and you will need to register your information online. This book includes access to the above resources for ONE PERSON ONLY.

To register and start using your online resources, please go online to the following URL:

http://www.manhattangmat.com/access.cfm   (Double check that you have typed this in accurately!)

Your one year of online access begins on the day that you register at the above URL. You only need to register your product ONCE at the above URL. To use your online resources any time AFTER you have completed the registration process, please login to the following URL:

http://www.manhattangmat.com/practicecenter.cfm

---

1. ALGEBRAIC TRANSLATIONS — 11

In Action Problems — 21
Solutions — 23

2. RATES & WORK — 29

In Action Problems — 45
Solutions — 47

3. RATIOS — 53

In Action Problems — 59
Solutions — 61

4. COMBINATORICS — 65

In Action Problems — 79
Solutions — 81

5. PROBABILITY — 89

In Action Problems — 101
Solutions — 103

6. STATISTICS — 109

In Action Problems — 121
Solutions — 123

7. OVERLAPPING SETS — 125

In Action Problems — 135
Solutions — 137

8. MINOR PROBLEM TYPES — 141

In Action Problems — 147
Solutions — 149

9. STRATEGIES FOR DATA SUFFICIENCY — 153

Sample Data Sufficiency Rephrasing — 157

10. OFFICIAL GUIDE PROBLEM SETS — 163

Problem Solving List — 166
Data Sufficiency List — 167

TABLE OF CONTENTS

g

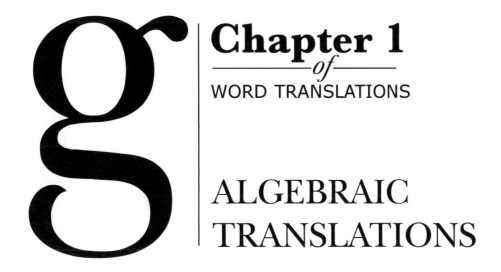

Chapter 1
of
WORD TRANSLATIONS

ALGEBRAIC TRANSLATIONS

In This Chapter . . .

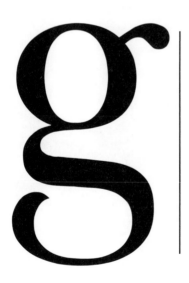

- Algebraic Translations
- Translating Words Correctly
- Using Charts to Organize Variables
- Prices and Quantities
- Hidden Constraints

Algebraic Translations

To solve many word problems on the GMAT, you must be able to translate English into algebra. You select variables and variable expressions to represent unknown quantities. Then you write equations to state relationships between the unknowns and any known values. Once you have written one or more algebraic equations to represent a problem, you can solve them to find any missing information.

> A candy company sells premium chocolates at $5 per pound and regular chocolates at $4 per pound. If Barrett buys a 7-pound box of chocolates that costs him $31, how many pounds of premium chocolates are in the box?

To solve this problem, simply translate the words into algebraic equations:

Step 1: Assign variables.
If possible, designate only one variable, and use it to represent all unknown information.

Almost every word problem will refer to more than one quantity, but most solutions work best when they involve only one variable. Therefore, you should try to express all quantities in terms of a single variable—ideally, the "Ultimate Unknown" that the problem is asking for, but only if that Ultimate Unknown is a simple quantity.

In the problem above, the pounds of premium and regular chocolate must add to 7. Therefore, if you know one of the weights in pounds, you can subtract from 7 to find the other. We can assign the following:

$$p \quad = \text{number of pounds of premium chocolate}$$
$$7 - p \quad = \text{number of pounds of regular chocolate}$$

You should also note that p is the Ultimate Unknown that the problem wants you to find. A good way to remind yourself is to write down "$p = ?$" on your paper.

Time is short during the GMAT, so you should not waste valuable seconds searching for one-variable expressions if you cannot nail them down right away. Instead, try using additional variables—but with an eye to finding substitutions that will ultimately reduce the number of variables to just one. In the chocolate problem, you could assign the following:

$$p \quad = \text{number of pounds of premium chocolate}$$
$$r \quad = \text{number of pounds of regular chocolate}$$

These two variables are related by the equation $p + r = 7$. Since the question is ultimately about p, you want a substitution that will eliminate r. Therefore, solve this equation for r:

$$r = 7 - p$$

Thus, there are p pounds of premium chocolate and $7 - p$ pounds of regular chocolate, and the problem has been successfully reduced to one variable. By the way, you *could* have used the letters x and y to represent the pounds of premium and regular chocolate, but if you use p and r, you will never forget which is which. Use meaningful letters if you can.

Be sure to make a note of what each variable represents. If you can, use meaningful letters as variable names.

<u>Step 2: Write equation(s).</u>
If you are not sure how to construct the equation, begin by expressing a relationship between the unknowns and the known values in **words**. For example, you might say:

"The total cost of the box is equal to the cost of the premium chocolates plus the cost of the regular chocolates."

You *might* even write down a "Word Equation," halfway between English and algebra:

"Total Cost of Box = Cost of Premiums + Cost of Regulars"

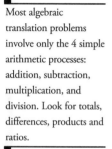

Most algebraic translation problems involve only the 4 simple arithmetic processes: addition, subtraction, multiplication, and division. Look for totals, differences, products and ratios.

Then, translate the verbal relationship into mathematical symbols. Use another relationship, *Total Cost = Unit Price × Quantity*, to write the terms on the right hand side. For instance, the "Cost of Premiums" in dollars = ($5 per pound)($p$ pounds) = $5p$.

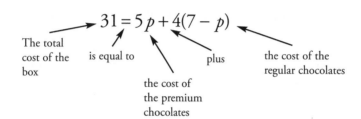

$$31 = 5p + 4(7 - p)$$

The total cost of the box   is equal to   plus   the cost of the regular chocolates

the cost of the premium chocolates

Note that many word problems, including this one, require a little basic background knowledge to complete the translation to algebra. Here, to write the expressions $5p$ and $4(7 - p)$, you must understand that *Total Cost = Unit Price × Quantity*. In this particular problem, the quantities are weights, and the units of those quantities are pounds.

Although the GMAT requires little factual knowledge, it will assume that you have mastered the following relationships:
- Total Cost = Unit Price × Quantity purchased
- Total Sales or Revenue = Unit Price × Quantity sold (essentially the same relation)
- Profit = Revenue − Cost
- Distance = Rate × Time (this relation will be covered in the next chapter)

<u>Step 3: Solve algebraically.</u>
$$31 = 5p + 4(7 - p)$$
$$31 = 5p + 28 - 4p$$
$$3 = p$$

<u>Step 4: Evaluate the algebraic solution in the context of the problem.</u>
Once you solve for the unknown, look back at the problem and make sure you answer the question asked. In this problem, we are asked for the number of pounds of premium chocolate in the box. This is the Ultimate Unknown. Notice that we wisely chose our variable p to represent the Ultimate Unknown. This way, once we have solved for p, there are no additional steps to take. If you use two variables, p and r, and accidentally solve for r instead of p, you might choose 4 as your answer. This is why you should always note what the Ultimate Unknown is at the beginning of the problem (e.g., by writing "$p = ?$").

*Manhattan*GMAT*Prep
the new standard

Translating Words Correctly

When you write equations representing relationships between variables—even if those relationships are fairly simple—you must be careful to **avoid writing the relationships backwards**. For instance, if you see "*A* is half the size of *B*," you should write $A = \dfrac{B}{2}$, not the wrong way around as $\dfrac{A}{2} = B$. Likewise, "*A* is 5 less than *B*" is written as $A = B - 5$. This relation is often incorrectly represented as $A = 5 - B$ or as $A - 5 = B$.

Because the stakes are so high for each GMAT problem, it is often worth a **quick check with easy numbers** to see whether you have written a relationship in the correct direction. For example, if you see "*A* is 5 less than *B*," then select, say, $A = 2$ and $B = 7$ to satisfy that relationship. (Note that these numbers do not have to satisfy other conditions given in the problem; their only purpose is to test the relationship you are looking at.) Trying these numbers in each of the three different re-writings of the equation yields

$A = B - 5$	➜	$2 = 7 - 5$	Correct!
$A = 5 - B$	➜	$2 = 5 - 7$?	Incorrect!
$A - 5 = B$	➜	$2 - 5 = 7$?	Incorrect!

Be ready to insert simple test numbers to make sure that your translation is correct.

This quick testing will confirm that you have indeed written the correct form of an equation, so that you can proceed with confidence. If you ever make these types of errors, then take the time to perform these quick tests. Many incorrect answer choices on the GMAT are derived from mistakes just like these!

Note also the **two uses of "less than."**

"*A* is 5 less than *B*" turns into an equation with a subtraction: $A = B - 5$
"*A* is less than *B*" turns into an inequality: $A < B$

The difference is whether you specify *how much* less than. "More than" works similarly.

Percents can be tricky:

"*p* is what percent of *q*?" turns into an equation with a new variable: $p = \left(\dfrac{x}{100}\right)q$.

Or you can write proportions: $\dfrac{p}{q} = \dfrac{x}{100}$. Either way, you need to solve for *x*.

Finally, note that not all statements should be translated one word or phrase at a time. Some translations require you to **view the statement *as a whole*** to write an appropriate equation. For instance, if you see "Justina bought twice as many apples as bananas at the market," then you should write $A = 2B$, **not** $2A = B$ (as you can check with easy numbers).

If you try to translate the equation word for word, you might get the incorrect version, because the word "twice" appears closer to "apples." Or you might wrongly think that $2A$ means "two apples." *A* represents the *number* of apples, which is *larger* than the number of bananas, *B*. So we must multiply the number of bananas by 2 to get the number of apples: $A = 2B$ is correct. The moral is this: always pay attention to the *meaning* of the sentence you are translating!

ALGEBRAIC TRANSLATIONS STRATEGY

Using Charts to Organize Variables

When an algebraic translation problem involves several quantities and multiple relationships, it is often a good idea to make a chart to organize information.

One type of algebraic translation that appears on the GMAT is the "age problem." Age problems ask you to find the age of an individual at a certain point in time, given some information about other people's ages at other times.

Complicated age problems can be effectively solved using an Age Chart. Such a chart helps you keep track of one person's age at different times or several ages at one time.

> 8 years ago, George was half as old as Sarah. Sarah is now 20 years older than George. How old will George be 10 years from now?

> The age chart does not relate the ages of the individuals. It simply helps you to assign variables you can use to write equations.

Step 1: Assign variables.

Set up an Age Chart to help you keep track of the quantities. Put the different people in rows and the different times in columns. Then assign variables. You could use two variables (G and S), or you could use just one variable (G) and represent Sarah's age as $G + 20$, since we are told that Sarah is now 20 years older than George. We will use the second approach. Either way, always use the variables to indicate the age of each person *now* (this way, you will not confuse yourself). Fill in the other columns by adding or subtracting time from the "now" column (for instance, subtract 8 to get the "8 years ago" column). Also note the Ultimate Unknown with a question mark.

	8 years ago	Now	10 years from now
George	$G - 8$	G	$G + 10 = ?$
Sarah	$G + 12$	$G + 20$	$G + 30$

Step 2: Write equation(s).

Write equations that relate the individuals' ages together. According to this problem, 8 years ago, George was half as old as Sarah. Using the age expressions in the "8 years ago" column, we can write the following equation:

$$G - 8 = \frac{G + 12}{2}$$ which can be rewritten as $2G - 16 = G + 12$

Step 3: Solve algebraically.

$$2G - 16 = G + 12$$
$$G = 28$$

Step 4: Evaluate the algebraic solution in the context of the problem.

In this problem, we are asked to find George's age in 10 years. In other words, $G + 10$ is the Ultimate Unknown. Since George is now 28 years old, he will be 38 in 10 years. The answer is 38 years.

Note that if we had used two variables, G and S, we might have set the table up slightly faster, but then we would have had to solve a system of 2 equations and 2 unknowns.

Prices and Quantities

Many GMAT word problems involve the total price or value of a mixed set of goods. On such problems, you should be able to write two different types of equations right away.

1. Relate the *quantities* or numbers of different goods: Sum of these numbers = Total.
2. Relate the total *values* of the goods (or their total cost, or the revenue from their sale):
   Money spent on one good = Price × Quantity.
   Sum of money spent on all goods = Total Value.

The following example could be the prompt of a Data Sufficiency problem:

> Paul has twenty-five transit cards, each worth either $5, $3, or $1.50. What is the total monetary value of all of Paul's transit cards?

Step 1. Define variables
There are three quantities in the problem, so the most obvious way to proceed is to designate a separate variable for each quantity:

x = number of $5 transit cards
y = number of $3 transit cards
z = number of $1.50 transit cards

Alternatively, you could use the given *relationship* between the three quantities (they sum to 25) to reduce the number of variables from three to two:

number of $5 transit cards = x
number of $3 transit cards = y
number of $1.50 transit cards = $25 - x - y$ or $25 - (x + y)$

Note that in both cases, the Ultimate Unknown (the total value of the cards) is *not* given a variable name. This total value is not a simple quantity; we will express it *in terms of* the variables we have defined.

Step 2. Write equations
If you use three variables, then you should write two equations. One equation relates the *quantities* or numbers of different transit cards; the other relates the *values* of the cards.
Numbers of cards: $x + y + z = 25$
Values of cards: $5x + 3y + 1.50z = ?$ (this is the Ultimate Unknown for the problem)

If you have trouble writing these equations, you can use a table to help you. The **columns** of the table are *Unit Price*, *Quantity*, and *Total Value* (with *Unit Price × Quantity = Total Value*). The **rows** correspond to the different types of items in the problem, with one additional row for *Total*.

In the *Quantity* and *Total Value* columns, but not in the *Unit Price* column, the individual rows sum to give the quantity in the *Total* row. Note that *Total Value* is a quantity of money (usually dollars), corresponding either to *Total Revenue*, *Total Cost*, or even *Total Profit*, depending on the problem's wording.

In a typical Price–Quantity problem, you have two relationships. The quantities sum to a total, and the monetary values sum to a total.

For this type of problem, you can save time by writing the equations directly. But feel free to use a table approach.

	Unit Price	×	Quantity	=	Total Value
$5 cards	5	×	x	=	5x
$3 cards	3	×	y	=	3y
$1.50 cards	1.5	×	z	=	1.5z
Total	—		25		?

You can use a table to organize your approach to a Price–Quantity problem. However, if you learn to write the equations directly, you will save time.

Notice that the numbers in the second and third columns of the table (*Quantity* and *Total Value*) can be added up to make a meaningful total, but the numbers in the first column (*Unit Price*) do not add up in any meaningful way.

If you use the two-variable approach, you do not need to write an equation relating the *numbers* of transit cards, because you have already used that relationship to write the expression for the number of $1.50 cards (as $25 - x - y$). Therefore, you only need to write the equation to sum up the values of the cards.

Values of cards: $5x + 3y + 1.50(25 - x - y) = ?$
Simplify $\rightarrow$ $3.5x + 1.5y + 37.5 = ?$

Here is the corresponding table:

	Unit Value	×	Quantity	=	Total Value
$5 cards	5	×	x	=	5x
$3 cards	3	×	y	=	3y
$1.50 cards	1.5	×	$25 - x - y$	=	$1.5(25 - x - y)$
Total	—		25		?

All of the work so far has come just from the *prompt* of a Data Sufficiency question—you have not even seen statements (1) and (2) yet! But this work is worth the time and energy. In general, you should rephrase and interpret a Data Sufficiency question prompt as much as you can before you begin to work with the statements.

Hidden Constraints

Notice that in the previous problem, there is a **hidden constraint** on the possible quantities of cards (x, y, and either z or $25 - x - y$). Since each card is a physical, countable object, you can only have a **whole number** of each type of card. Whole numbers are the integers 0, 1, 2, and so on. So you can have 1 card, 2 cards, 3 cards, etc., and even 0 cards, but you cannot have fractional cards or negative cards.

As a result of this implied "whole number" constraint, you actually have more information than you might think. Thus, you may be able to answer the question with less information from the statements.

As an extreme example, imagine that the question is "What is x?" and that statement (1) reads "$1.9 < x < 2.2$". If some constraint (hidden or not) restricts x to whole-number values, then statement (1) is sufficient to answer the question: x must equal 2. On the other hand, without constraints on x, statement (1) is not sufficient to determine what x is.

Recognizing a hidden constraint can be useful, not only on Data Sufficiency problems, but also on certain Problem Solving problems. Consider the following example:

> If Kelly received 1/3 more votes than Mike in a student election, which of the
> following could have been the total number of votes cast for the two candi-
> dates?
>
> (A) 12
> (B) 13
> (C) 14
> (D) 15
> (E) 16

Let M be the number of votes cast for Mike. Then Kelly received $M + (1/3)M$, or $(4/3)M$ votes. The total number of votes cast was therefore "votes for Mike" plus "votes for Kelly," or $M + (4/3)M$. This quantity equals $(7/3)M$, or $7M/3$.

Because M is a number of votes, it cannot be a fraction—specifically, not a fraction with a 7 in the denominator. Therefore, the 7 in the expression $7M/3$ cannot be cancelled out. As a result, the total number of votes cast must be a multiple of 7. Among the answer choices, the only multiple of 7 is 14, so the correct answer is (**C**).

Another way to solve this problem is this: the number of votes cast for Mike (M) must be a multiple of 3, since the total number of votes is a whole number. So $M = 3, 6, 9$, etc. Kelly received 1/3 more votes, so the number of votes she received is 4, 8, 12, etc. Thus the total number of votes is 7, 14, 21, etc.

Not every unknown quantity related to real objects is restricted to whole numbers. Many physical measurements, such as weights, times, or speeds, can be any positive number, not necessarily integers. A few quantities can even be negative (e.g., temperatures, x- or y-coordinates). Think about what is being measured or counted, and you will recognize whether a hidden constraint applies.

When a variable indicates how many objects there are, it must be a whole number.

Problem Set

Solve the following problems with the four-step method outlined in this section.

1.   John is 20 years older than Brian. 12 years ago, John was twice as old as Brian. How old is Brian?

2.   Mrs. Miller has two dogs, Jackie and Stella, who weigh a total of 75 pounds. If Stella weighs 15 pounds less than twice Jackie's weight, how much does Stella weigh?

3.   Caleb spends $72.50 on 50 hamburgers for the marching band. If single burgers cost $1.00 each and double burgers cost $1.50 each, how many double burgers did he buy?

4.   Abigail is 4 times as old as Bonnie. In 6 years, Bonnie will be twice as old as Candice. If, 4 years from now, Abigail will be 36 years old, how old will Candice be in 6 years?

5.   United Telephone charges a base rate of $10.00 for service, plus an additional charge of $0.25 per minute. Atlantic Call charges a base rate of $12.00 for service, plus an additional charge of $0.20 per minute. For what number of minutes would the bills for each telephone company be the same?

6.   Ross is 3 times as old as Sam, and Sam is 3 years older than Tina. 2 years from now, Tina will drink from the Fountain of Youth, which will cut her age in half. If after drinking from the Fountain, Tina is 16 years old, how old is Ross right now?

7.   Carina has 100 ounces of coffee divided into 5- and 10-ounce packages. If she has 2 more 5-ounce packages than 10-ounce packages, how many 10-ounce packages does she have?

8.   Carla cuts a 70-inch piece of ribbon into 2 pieces. If the first piece is five inches more than one fourth as long as the second piece, how long is the longer piece of ribbon?

9.   In a used car lot, there are 3 times as many red cars as green cars. If tomorrow 12 green cars are sold and 3 red cars are added, then there will be 6 times as many red cars as green cars. How many green cars are currently in the lot?

10.   Jane started baby-sitting when she was 18 years old. Whenever she baby-sat for a child, that child was no more than half her age at the time. Jane is currently 32 years old, and she stopped baby-sitting 10 years ago. What is the current age of the oldest person for whom Jane could have baby-sat?

11.   If Brianna triples her money at blackjack and then leaves a ten-dollar tip for the dealer, she will leave the casino with the same amount of money as if she had won 190 dollars at roulette. How much money did Brianna take into the casino?

12.   Martin buys a pencil and a notebook for 80 cents. At the same store, Gloria buys a notebook and an eraser for $1.20, and Zachary buys a pencil and an eraser for 70 cents. How much would it cost to buy three pencils, three notebooks, and three erasers? (Assume that there is no volume discount.)

13.   Andrew will be half as old as Larry in 3 years. Andrew will also be one-third as old as Jerome in 5 years. If Jerome is 15 years older than Larry, how old is Andrew?

14.   A circus earned $150,000 in ticket revenue by selling 1,800 V.I.P. and Standard tickets. They sold 25% more Standard tickets than V.I.P. tickets. If the revenue from Standard tickets represents a third of the total ticket revenue, what is the price of a V.I.P. ticket?

15.   8 years from now, the bottle of wine labeled "Aged" will be 7 times as old the bottle of wine labeled "Table." 1 year ago, the bottle of wine labeled "Table" was one-fourth as old as the bottle of wine labeled "Vintage." If the "Aged" bottle was 20 times as old as the "Vintage" bottle 2 years ago, then how old is each bottle now?

1. **32:** Use an age chart to assign variables. Represent Brian's age now with b. Then John's age now is $b + 20$.

	12 years ago	Now
John	$b + 8$	$b + 20$
Brian	$b - 12$	$b = ?$

Subtract 12 from the "now" column to get the "12 years ago" column.

Then write an equation to represent the remaining information: 12 years ago, John was twice as old as Brian. Solve for b:

$$b + 8 = 2(b - 12)$$
$$b + 8 = 2b - 24$$
$$32 = b$$

You could also solve this problem by inspection. John is 20 years older than Brian. We also need John to be *twice* Brian's age at a particular point in time. Since John is always 20 years older, then he must be 40 years old at that time (and Brian must be 20 years old). This point in time was 12 years ago, so Brian is now 32 years old.

2. **45 pounds:**
Let j = Jackie's weight, and let s = Stella's weight. Stella's weight is the Ultimate Unknown: $s = ?$

The two dogs weigh a total of 75 pounds.   Stella weighs 15 pounds less than twice Jackie's weight.
$$j + s = 75 \qquad\qquad s = 2j - 15$$

Combine the two equations by substituting the value for s from equation (2) into equation (1).
$$j + (2j - 15) = 75$$
$$3j - 15 = 75$$
$$3j = 90$$
$$j = 30$$

Find Stella's weight by substituting Jackie's weight into equation (1).
$$30 + s = 75$$
$$s = 45$$

3. **45 double burgers:**
> Let s = the number of single burgers purchased
> Let d = the number of double burgers purchased

Caleb bought 50 burgers: Caleb spent \$72.50 in all:
$$s + d = 50 \qquad\qquad s + 1.5d = 72.50$$

Combine the two equations by subtracting equation (1) from equation (2).
$$\begin{aligned} s + 1.5d &= 72.50 \\ -(s + \quad d &= 50) \\ \hline 0.5d &= 22.5 \\ d &= 45 \end{aligned}$$

4. 7: First, set up a blank age chart for the three people and the three points in time. We could make up three variables (*a, b,* and *c*) for the three current ages, but then we would have to solve a system of 3 equations and 3 unknowns. It is simpler to create one variable and then take it as far as we can go.

	Now	in 4 years	in 6 years
Abigail			
Bonnie			
Candice			

Let us take the first piece of information: Abigail is 4 times as old as Bonnie. If we let *b* stand for Bonnie's age now, then Abigail's age is 4*b*. Put these two expressions into the chart.

	Now	in 4 years	in 6 years
Abigail	4*b*		
Bonnie	*b*		
Candice			

Next, in 6 years, Bonnie will be twice as old as Candice. We write *b* + 6 for Bonnie's age in 6 years. Since that number is twice Candice's age then, Candice's age will be (*b* + 6)/2.

	Now	in 4 years	in 6 years
Abigail	4*b*		
Bonnie	*b*		*b* + 6
Candice			(*b* + 6)/2

Finally, 4 years from now, Abigail will be 36 years old. We can now solve for *b*:

$$4b + 4 = 36$$
$$b = 8$$

Substitute this value into the expression for Candice's age in 6 years:

$$(b + 6)/2 = (8 + 6)/2 = 7$$

	Now	in 4 years	in 6 years
Abigail	4*b*	4*b* + 4	
Bonnie	*b*		*b* + 6
Candice			(*b* + 6)/2

5. 40 minutes:
Let *x* = the number of minutes
A call made by United Telephone costs $10.00 plus $0.25 per minute: 10 + 0.25*x*.
A call made by Atlantic Call costs $12.00 plus $0.20 per minute: 12 + 0.20*x*.

Set the expressions equal to each other:

$$10 + 0.25x = 12 + 0.20x$$
$$0.05x = 2$$
$$x = 40$$

6. 99: Set up an age chart. Again, we could make up three variables (*r, s,* and *t*) for the three current ages, but it is simpler to create one variable.

	Now	in 2 years
Ross		
Sam		
Tina		

Sam's age is given in terms of Tina's age, and Ross's age is given in terms of Sam's age. Thus, it is easiest to create *t* to stand for Tina's age now. Since Sam is 3 years older than Tina, we insert *t* + 3 for Sam's age now. Then Ross is 3 times as old as Sam, so we insert 3(*t* + 3) = 3*t* + 9 for Ross's age now. Finally, we have Tina's age in 2 years as *t* + 2. In 2 years, Tina's age (magically cut in half) will be 16: $\dfrac{t+2}{2} = 16$.

	Now	in 2 years
Ross	3*t* + 9 = ?	
Sam	*t* + 3	
Tina	*t*	*t* + 2

Work backwards to solve the problem:

$$t + 2 = 32 \qquad t = 30 \qquad$$ Thus, Ross's age right now is 3*t* + 9 = 3(30) + 9 = 99.

*Manhattan*GMAT*Prep
the new standard

7. **6:**

> Let a = the number of 5-ounce packages
> Let b = the number of 10-ounce packages

Carina has 100 ounces of coffee: She has two more 5-ounce packages than 10-ounce packages:

$5a + 10b = 100$ $a = b + 2$

Combine the equations by substituting the value of a from equation (2) into equation (1).

$$5(b+2)+10b = 100$$
$$5b+10+10b = 100$$
$$15b+10 = 100$$
$$15b = 90$$
$$b = 6$$

8. **52 inches:**

> Let x = the 1st piece of ribbon
> Let y = the 2nd piece of ribbon

The ribbon is 70 inches long.   The 1st piece is 5 inches more than 1/4 as long as the 2nd.

$$x + y = 70$$ $$x = 5 + \frac{y}{4}$$

Combine the equations by substituting the value of x from equation (2) into equation (1):

$$5+\frac{y}{4}+y = 70$$
$$20+y+4y = 280$$
$$5y = 260$$
$$y = 52 \quad \text{Now, since } x+y=70, x=18. \text{ This tells us that } x < y, \text{ so } y \text{ is the answer.}$$

9. **25:**

Set up a quick chart, and let g = the number of green cars today. Then the number of red cars today is $3g$ ("there are 3 times as many red cars as green cars"). Tomorrow, we add 3 red cars and remove 12 green cars, leading to the expressions in the "tomorrow" column. Finally, we write an equation to represent the fact that there will be 6 times as many red cars as green cars tomorrow.

$$3g+3 = 6(g-12) = 6g-72$$
$$3g = 75$$
$$g = 25$$

	Now	Tomorrow
Green	g	$g - 12$
Red	$3g$	$3g + 3$

10. **23:** Since you are given actual ages for Jane, the easiest way to solve the problem is to think about the extreme scenarios. At one extreme, 18-year-old Jane could have baby-sat a child of age 9. Since Jane is now 32, that child would now be 23. At the other extreme, 22-year-old Jane could have baby-sat a child of age 11. Since Jane is now 32 that child would now be 21. We can see that the first scenario yields the oldest possible current age (23) of a child that Jane baby-sat.

11. $100:

Let x = the amount of money Brianna took into the casino

If Brianna triples her money and then leaves a ten-dollar tip, she will have $3x - 10$ dollars left. If she had won 190 dollars, she would have had $x + 190$ dollars.

Set these two amounts equal to each other:

$$3x - 10 = x + 190$$
$$2x = 200$$
$$x = 100$$

12. $4.05:

Let p = price of 1 pencil
Let n = price of 1 notebook
Let e = price of 1 eraser

Martin buys a pencil and a notebook for 80 cents: $\qquad p + n \qquad = 80$

Gloria buys a notebook and an eraser for $1.20, or 120 cents: $\qquad n + e = 120$

Zachary buys a pencil and an eraser for 70 cents: $\qquad p \qquad + e = 70$

One approach would be to solve for the variables separately. However, notice that the Ultimate Unknown is not the price of any individual item but rather the *combined* price of 3 pencils, 3 notebooks, and 3 erasers. In algebraic language, we can write

$$3p + 3n + 3e = 3(p + n + e) = ?$$

Thus, if we can find the sum of the three prices quickly, we can simply multiply by 3 and have the answer.

The three equations we are given are very similar to each other. It should occur to us to add up all the equations:

$$
\begin{aligned}
p + n \qquad &= 80 \\
n + e &= 120 \\
\underline{p \qquad + e} &= \underline{70} \\
2p + 2n + 2e &= 270
\end{aligned}
$$

We are now close to the Ultimate Unknown. All we need to do is multiply both sides by $\dfrac{3}{2}$:

$$\left(\frac{3}{2}\right)(2p + 2n + 2e) = 270\left(\frac{3}{2}\right) = \cancel{270}135\left(\frac{3}{\cancel{2}}\right) = 405$$
$$3p + 3n + 3e = 405$$

13. **8:** Set up a blank age chart with 3 rows for the different people and 3 columns for the different points in time.

	Now	in 3 years	in 5 years
Andrew			
Larry			
Jerome			

Next, to decide how to name variables, consider the first two pieces of information given:
(1) Andrew will be 1/2 as old as Larry in 3 years.
(2) Andrew will be 1/3 as old as Jerome in 5 years.
Since Andrew is the common element, and since A is the Ultimate Unknown, we should name Andrew's current age A and see how far we can go with just one variable.

	Now	in 3 years	in 5 years
Andrew	$A = ?$		
Larry			
Jerome			

(1) Andrew will be 1/2 as old as Larry in 3 years. At that time, Andrew's age will be $A + 3$. Since he will be 1/2 as old as Larry, Larry will be *twice* his age. So we can represent Larry's age in 3 years as $2(A + 3) = 2A + 6$.

	Now	in 3 years	in 5 years
Andrew	$A = ?$	$A + 3$	
Larry		$2A + 6$	
Jerome			

(2) Andrew will be 1/3 as old as Jerome in 5 years. At that time, Andrew's age will be $A + 5$. Since he will be 1/3 as old as Jerome, Jerome will be *3 times* his age. So we can represent Jerome's age in 5 years as $3(A + 5) = 3A + 15$.

	Now	in 3 years	in 5 years
Andrew	$A = ?$	$A + 3$	$A + 5$
Larry		$2A + 6$	
Jerome			$3A + 15$

The last piece of information is this: Jerome is 15 years older than Larry. So we need to have expressions for Larry's age and Jerome's age *at the same time*. It is probably easiest conceptually to bring both future ages back to the present. We subtract 3 from Larry's future age (in 3 years), yielding $2A + 3$ for Larry's current age. Likewise, we subtract 5 from Jerome's future age, yielding $3A + 10$ for Jerome's current age.

	Now	in 3 years	in 5 years
Andrew	$A = ?$	$A + 3$	$A + 5$
Larry	$2A + 3$	$2A + 6$	
Jerome	$3A + 10$		$3A + 15$

Finally, we write the relationship between Larry's current age and Jerome's current age (Jerome is 15 years older), and we solve for A:

$$\text{Larry} + 15 = \text{Jerome}$$
$$(2A + 3) + 15 = 3A + 10 \quad \rightarrow \quad 2A + 18 = 3A + 10 \quad \rightarrow \quad 8 = A$$

14. **$125:** Because this problem conflates Price-Quantity equations with fractions and percentages, it is helpful to make a table to organize all the information given. This will help you establish which information is unknown, so you can assign variables. If we call the number of VIP tickets n, then the number of Standard tickets is 25% more than n, which is $n + (25\% \text{ of } n) = n + 0.25n = 1.25n$. Since the revenue from Standard tickets represents 1/3 of the total ticket revenue of $150,000, we can fill in $50,000 for the revenue from Standard tickets and $100,000 (the remainder) as revenue from VIP tickets.

	Unit Value	×	*Quantity*	=	*Total Value*
VIP	v	×	n	=	100,000
Standard	s	×	$1.25n$	=	50,000
Total	—	×	1,800	=	150,000

You know that there were a total of 1,800 tickets sold. Using this information, solve for n and update the chart as follows:

$$n + 1.25n = 1,800$$
$$2.25n = 1,800$$
$$n = 800$$

	Unit Value		Quantity		Total Value
VIP	v	×	**800**	=	100,000
Standard	s	×	**1,000**	=	50,000
Total	—	×	**1,800**	=	150,000

Lastly, solve for v: $800v = 100,000$
$v = 125$

(For more detailed information on percentage increases and related topics, see the Manhattan GMAT *Fractions, Decimals, and Percents* Strategy Guide.)

15. **Table – 2 years old; Aged – 62 years old; Vintage – 5 years old:**

Set up an age chart to assign variables. In theory we could make up 3 variables, but to simplify matters, we should make up one variable and see how far we can go. Let t be the current age of the Table wine.
We fill in the rest of the row by adding and subtracting time.

	2 years ago	1 year ago	Now	in 8 years
Aged				
Table	$t-2$	$t-1$	t	$t+8$
Vintage				

Now fill in other information. First of all, 8 years from now, Aged will be 7 times as old as Table. Also, one year ago, Table was one-fourth as old as Vintage. This means that Vintage was *four times* as old as Table, one year ago.

	2 years ago	1 year ago	Now	in 8 years
Aged				$7t+56$
Table	$t-2$	$t-1$	t	$t+8$
Vintage		$4t-4$		

Now, fill in the "2 years ago" column by subtracting time.

	2 years ago	1 year ago	Now	in 8 years
Aged	$7t+46$			$7t+56$
Table	$t-2$	$t-1$	t	$t+8$
Vintage	$4t-5$	$4t-4$		

Finally, we express the last relationship: 2 years ago, Aged was 20 times as old as Vintage.

$$7t + 46 = 20(4t - 5) = 80t - 100 \quad \rightarrow \quad 146 = 73t \quad \rightarrow \quad 2 = t$$

Now, fill in the rest of the "Now" column and find the other current ages.

	2 years ago	1 year ago	Now	in 8 years
Aged	$7t+46$		$7t+48$	$7t+56$
Table	$t-2$	$t-1$	$t=2$	$t+8$
Vintage	$4t-5$	$4t-4$	$4t-3$	

Aged Now = $7t + 48$
Aged Now = $7(2) + 48$
Aged Now = 62

Vintage Now = $4t - 3$
Vintage Now = $4(2) - 3$
Vintage Now = 5

ManhattanGMAT Prep
the new standard

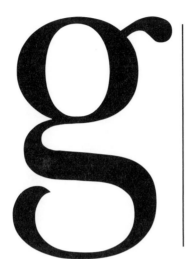

Chapter 2
of
WORD TRANSLATIONS

RATES & WORK

In This Chapter . . .

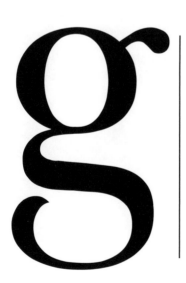

- Basic Motion: The RTD Chart
- Matching Units in the RTD Chart
- Multiple RTD Problems
- Average Rate: Don't Just Add and Divide
- Basic Work Problems
- Working Together: Add the Rates
- Population Problems
- Equations for Exponential Growth or Decay (Advanced)

RATES & WORK

The GMAT's favorite Word Translation type is the RATE problem. Rate problems come in a variety of forms on the GMAT, but all are marked by three primary components: RATE, TIME, & DISTANCE or WORK.

These three elements are related by the equation:

$$\text{Rate} \times \text{Time} = \text{Distance}$$
$$\text{or} \quad \text{Rate} \times \text{Time} = \text{Work}$$

These equations can be abbreviated as $RT = D$ or as $RT = W$. Basic rate problems involve simple manipulations of these equations.

Note that rate-of-travel problems (with a physical distance) and work problems are really the same from the point of view of the math. The main difference is that for work problems, the right side of the equation is not a distance but an *output* (e.g., hamburgers cooked). Also, the rate is measured not in units of distance per unit of time (e.g., 10 miles per hour), but in units of *output* per unit of time (e.g., 5 hamburgers cooked per minute).

Rate problems on the GMAT come in five main forms:
  (1)   Basic Motion Problems
  (2)   Average Rate Problems
  (3)   Simultaneous Motion Problems
  (4)   Work Problems
  (5)   Population Problems

For simple motion problems, use the equation $RT = D$. Simply plug in the values you know and solve for the unknown.

Basic Motion: The RTD Chart

All basic motion problems involve three elements: Rate, Time, and Distance.

Rate is expressed as a ratio of distance and time, with two corresponding units.
Some examples of rates include: 30 miles per hour, 10 meters/second, 15 kilometers/day.

Time is expressed using one unit of time.
Some examples of times include: 6 hours, 23 seconds, 5 months, etc.

Distance is expressed using one unit of distance.
Some examples of distances include: 18 miles, 20 meters, 100 kilometers.

You can make an "RTD chart" to solve a basic motion problem. Read the problem and fill in two of the variables. Then use the $RT = D$ formula to find the missing variable.

> If a car is traveling at 30 miles per hour, how long does it take to travel 75 miles?

An RTD chart is shown to the right. Fill in your RTD chart with the given information. Then solve for the time:
$$30t = 75, \text{ or } t = 2.5 \text{ hours}$$

	Rate (mi/hr)	×	Time (hr)	=	Distance (mi)
Car	30 mi/hr	×		=	75 mi

Matching Units in the RTD Chart

It is imperative that all the units in your RTD chart match up with one another. The two units in the rate should match up with the unit of time and the unit of distance. For example:

> It takes an elevator four seconds to go up one floor. How many floors will the elevator rise in two minutes?

The rate is 1 floor/4 seconds, which simplifies to 0.25 floors/second. Note: the rate is NOT 4 seconds per floor! This is an extremely frequent error. Always express rates as "distance over time," not as "time over distance."

The time is 2 minutes. The distance is unknown.

Make units match before you substitute any values into $RT = D$ or $RT = W$.

	R (floors/sec)	×	T (min)	=	W (floors)
Elevator	0.25	×	2	=	?

Watch out! There is a problem with this RTD chart. The rate is expressed in floors per second, but the time is expressed in minutes. This will yield an incorrect answer.

To correct this table, we can change the time into seconds. Then all the units will match.

	R (floors/sec)	×	T (sec)	=	W (floors)
Elevator	0.25	×	120	=	?

The time has been converted from 2 minutes to 120 seconds. Now the time unit matches the rate unit, and we can solve for the distance using the $RT = D$ equation:

$$0.25(120) = d \qquad d = 30 \text{ floors}$$

Another example:

> A train travels 90 kilometers/hr. How many hours does it take the train to travel 450,000 meters?

Notice that before entering the information into the RTD chart, we convert the distance from 450,000 meters to 450 km. This is necessary so that the distance unit matches up with the rate, which is expressed in kilometers per hour.

	R (km/hr)	×	T (hr)	=	W (km)
Train	90	×	?	=	450

We can now solve for the time: $90t = 450$. Thus, $t = 5$ hours.

The RTD chart may seem like overkill for relatively simple problems such as these. In fact, for such problems, you can simply set up the equation $RT = D$ or $RT = W$ and then substitute. However, the RTD chart comes into its own when we have more complicated scenarios that contain more than one RTD relationship, as we see in the next section.

Multiple RTD Problems

Difficult GMAT rate problems often involve rates, times, and distances for *more than one trip or traveler*. For instance, you might have more than one person taking a trip, or you might have one person making multiple trips. We expand the RTD chart by adding rows for each trip. Sometimes, we also add a total row.

	Rate (miles/hour)	×	Time (hour)	=	Distance (miles)
Trip 1		×		=	
Trip 2		×		=	
Total					

For each trip, the rate, time, and distance work in the usual manner ($RT = D$), but you have additional relationships among the multiple trips. You will need to write these relationships mathematically. For instance, you might fill in *two* boxes in different rows with the same variable, or with expressions containing the same variable. Below is a list of typical relationships among the multiple trips or travelers.

RATE RELATIONS

Twice / half / n times as fast as

If train *A* is traveling at twice the speed of train *B*, then represent the speed of train *A* as $2r$ and the speed of train *B* as r. Do not reverse these expressions. If necessary, think of a quick pair of test numbers (e.g., if train *B* is going 50 miles per hour, then train *A* is going 100 miles per hour).

Slower / faster

If Wendy walks at a rate 1 mile per hour slower than Maurice's rate, then represent Maurice's rate as r and Wendy's as $r - 1$. Alternatively, you could represent Maurice's rate as $r + 1$ and Wendy's as r (depending if you are solving for Maurice or Wendy).

Relative rates

If two people are moving directly *toward* or *away from* each other, you *add* their rates to determine how fast the distance between them is changing. Imagine two cars heading toward each other. Car *A* is going 30 miles per hour; car *B* is going 40 miles per hour. The distance between the cars shrinks at a rate of 70 miles per hour. In algebraic terms: if car *A* is going *a* miles per hour and car B is going *b* miles per hour, then the distance between the cars shrinks at a rate of ($a + b$) miles per hour. If the cars are driving away from each other, then the distance grows at a rate of ($a + b$) miles per hour.

If the two cars are moving *in the same direction*, you *subtract* their rates to determine how fast the distance between them is changing. Imagine Car *B* chasing Car *A*. If Car *A* is going 40 miles per hour, but Car *B* (behind) is only going 30 miles per hour, then the gap grows at 10 miles per hour. If, instead, Car *B* is going 55 miles per hour, then the gap shrinks at 15 miles per hour. Algebraically, the distance between the cars changes at a rate of $|a - b|$ miles per hour. (We take the absolute value to make the relative rate positive.)

When you have more than one trip or traveler, make a row in your RTD chart for each trip.

TIME RELATIONS

Slower / faster

If Joey runs a race 30 seconds faster than Tommy, then represent Joey's time (in seconds) as $t - 30$ and Tommy's time as t. Alternatively, Joey's time can be represented as t and Tommy's as $t + 30$. These signs are the *opposites* of the ones for the "slower / faster" rate relations. If Joey runs a race faster than Tommy, then Joey's speed is higher, but his time is lower.

Left ... and met / arrived

If Sue and Tara left their original locations at the same time and then *met* somewhere, then they both traveled for the *same* amount of time. Thus, both their times can be written as t.

If Sue and Tara left their original locations at the same time, and Sun arrived at her destination one hour *before* Tara arrived at hers, then Sue's time can be represented as t and Tara's time as $t + 1$, or Sue's as $t - 1$ and Tara's as t. Tara traveled for one hour *longer* than Sue.

If Sue left her original location one hour *after* Tara left hers, and they *met* somewhere, then Sue's time can be represented as t and Tara's time as $t + 1$, or Sue's as $t - 1$ and Tara's as t. Again, Tara traveled for one hour longer than Sue.

Most Rate problems fit into one of several typical situations. Use these models as guidance.

SAMPLE SITUATIONS

The numbers in the same *row* of an RTD table will *always* multiply across: Rate × Time always equals Distance. However, the specifics of the problem determine which *columns* (R, T, and/or D) will add up into a total row.

The most common Multiple RTD situations are described below. Whenever you encounter a new Multiple RTD problem, try to make an analogy between the new problem and one of the following situations. For simplicity, we refer to "people" as the travelers throughout, but they could be cars, trains, airplanes, and so forth. The separate rows in your RTD chart should correspond to the different travelers, unless otherwise noted.

The Kiss: Two people travel toward each other and eventually meet.
RATES add to a combined rate (as described in the relative rates section).
TIMES do not add, but they are often the same for the two people (unless one starts earlier, in which case you write that person's time as t + the headstart).
DISTANCES add to the total distance traveled.

The Quarrel: Two people start at the same location and travel directly away from each other.
RATES add to a combined rate (as described in the relative rates section).
TIMES do not add, but they are often the same for the two people (unless one travels for a longer period of time after the split-up).
DISTANCES add to the total distance traveled.

The Chase: One person chases another, traveling in the same direction.
RATES subtract (as described in the relative rates section).
TIMES do not add, but they are often the same (unless one of the people starts earlier).
DISTANCES subtract. The difference represents the amount by which the "chaser" has caught up (if he or she is faster) or fallen further behind (if he or she is slower), so you might have to subtract this difference from, or add it to, the original gap.

Manhattan GMAT*Prep*
the new standard

Round Trip: One person travels a round trip. The rows in your RTD chart correspond to the two halves of the trip: "Going" and "Return."

RATES do not combine.

TIMES add down to a total time for the round trip.

DISTANCE is the same for each leg of the journey. Therefore, the total distance is twice the distance for each leg. Often, you can _make up_ a convenient value for the distance. Pick a Smart Number—a value that is a multiple of all the given rates or times.

Following footsteps: Two people travel the same path, but at different times.

RATES do not combine.

TIMES do not combine.

DISTANCE is the same for each person. Again, pick a Smart Number if necessary.

Second-guessing: A real trip is described, followed by statements about what _would_ have happened if the person had made the same journey faster, slower, etc. The rows in your RTD chart can be labeled as "Actual" and "Hypothetical."

RATES do not combine.

TIMES do not combine.

DISTANCES are the same for the actual and hypothetical trips. Again, pick a Smart Number if necessary.

No matter what situation exists in a problem, you will often have a choice as you name variables. When in doubt, use variables to stand for either Rate or Time, rather than Distance. This strategy will leave you with easier and faster calculations (products rather than ratios).

Use the following step-by-step method to solve Multiple RTD problems such as this:

> Stacy and Heather are 20 miles apart and walk towards each other along the same route. Stacy walks at a constant rate that is 1 mile per hour faster than Heather's constant rate of 5 miles/hour. If Heather starts her journey 24 minutes after Stacy, how far from her original destination has Heather walked when the two meet?
> (A) 7 miles (B) 8 miles (C) 9 miles (D) 10 miles (E) 12 miles

First, make sure that you understand the physical situation portrayed in the problem. The category is "The Kiss": two people walk toward each other and meet. Notice that Stacy starts walking first. If necessary, you might even draw a picture to clarify the scene.

Go ahead and convert any mismatched units. Because all the rates are given in miles per _hour_, you should convert the time that is given in _minutes_: $24 \text{ min} \times \dfrac{1 \text{ hr}}{60 \text{ min}} = 0.4 \text{ hr}$.

Now start setting up your RTD chart. Fill in all the numbers that you know or can compute very simply: Heather's speed is 5 miles/hour, and Stacy's speed is $5 + 1 = 6$ miles/hour. Next, you should try to introduce only _one variable_. If you introduce more than one variable, you will have to eliminate it later to solve the problem; this elimination can cost you valuable time. Let t stand for Heather's time. Also, we know that Stacy walked for 0.4 hours more than Heather, so Stacy's time is $t + 0.4$.

Label the rows in your RTD chart clearly. Notice what adds up and what does not for the type of problem at hand.

	Rate (mi/h)	×	Time (hr)	=	Distance (mi)
Stacy	6	×	$t + 0.4$	=	
Heather	5	×	t	=	
Total	—				20 mi

You can often approach Multiple RTD problems in more than one way. Choose an approach that works for you, but be sure to understand the others.

Finish the table by multiplying across rows (as always) and by adding the one column that *can* be added in this problem (distance).

	Rate (mi/h)	×	Time (hr)	=	Distance (mi)
Stacy	6	×	$t + 0.4$	=	**6t + 2.4** mi
Heather	5	×	t	=	**5t** mi
Total	—				20 mi

The table produces the equation $(6t + 2.4) + 5t = 20$, yielding $t = 1.6$. Heather's distance is therefore $5t$, or 8 miles.

Finally, notice that if you were stuck, you could have eliminated some wrong answer choices by thinking about the physical situation. Heather started later *and* walked more slowly; therefore, she cannot have covered half the 20 miles before Stacy reached her. Thus, answer choices D (10 miles) and E (12 miles) are impossible.

Alternate solution: Relative rate

You can simplify this problem by thinking further about the "Kiss" scenario. First, find the distance Stacy walks in the first 24 minutes (= 0.4 hours) by herself: $d = r \times t = (6$ mi/h$) \times (0.4$ h$) = 2.4$ mi. Therefore, once Heather starts walking, the two women have $20 - 2.4 = 17.6$ miles left to travel. Because the two women are now traveling for the *same time* in *opposite directions* (in this case, toward each other), you can just use the concept of relative rate: the distance between them is shrinking at the rate of $6 + 5 = 11$ miles per hour.

This idea of relative rates eliminates the need for two separate equations, leading to the simplified table shown at right. Solving the resulting equation gives $t = 1.6$ hours. This is the time during which both women are walking.

R (mi/hr)	×	T (hr)	=	D (mi)
11	×	t	=	17.6

Now set up another *simple* RTD table for Heather by herself.

R (mi/hr)	×	T (hr)	=	D (mi)
5	×	1.6	=	D

Heather's distance is therefore $5 \times 1.6 = 8$ miles.

The algebraic manipulations are actually very similar in both solutions, but the second approach is more intuitive, and the intermediate calculations make sense. By reformulating problems, you can often increase your understanding and your confidence, even if you do not save that much work.

*Manhattan*GMAT*Prep
the new standard

Consider another example.

> Liam is pulled over for speeding just as he is arriving at work. He explains to
> the police officer that he could not afford to be late today, and has arrived at
> work only four minutes before he is to start. The officer explains that if Liam
> had driven 5 mph slower for his whole commute, he would have arrived at
> work exactly on time. If Liam's commute is 30 miles long, how fast was he
> actually driving? (Assume that Liam drove at a constant speed for the dura-
> tion of his commute.)

This is a "Second-Guessing" problem, which presents the *actual* data about a completed trip
alongside *hypothetical* data about the same trip under different circumstances. Because the
route is the same for both trips, the distances (actual and hypothetical) must be equal.

Note the mismatched units: the difference in times is given in minutes, while all other time
units in the problem are hours. Therefore, change the 4 minutes to hours:

$$4 \text{ min} \times \frac{1 \text{ hr}}{60 \text{ min}} = \frac{1}{15} \text{hr}$$

The given *rate relationship* tells you that the actual speed is 5 mph *faster* than the hypothetical speed, so define those speeds as $r + 5$ and r respectively. Then make the RTD chart:

	Rate (mi/h)	×	Time (h)	=	Distance (mi)
Actual	$r + 5$	×	$\dfrac{30}{r+5}$	=	30
Hypothetical	r	×	$\dfrac{30}{r}$	=	30

Use the chart to write the expressions for the times (shown in boldface as fractions). Since
the hypothetical trip takes exactly 1/15 hour (= four minutes) longer than the actual trip,
set up an equation to relate the actual and hypothetical times:

$$\frac{30}{r} = \frac{30}{r+5} + \frac{1}{15}$$

Now the task is algebraic. We should note that in any real GMAT problem, you could plug
answer choices at this point. First, add the fractions by making a common denominator:

$$\frac{30}{r} = \frac{(15)(30)}{15(r+5)} + \frac{r+5}{15(r+5)} = \frac{450}{15(r+5)} + \frac{r+5}{15(r+5)}$$

$$\frac{30}{r} = \frac{r+455}{15(r+5)}$$

Now cross multiply:

$$(30)(15)(r+5) = r^2 + 455r$$

$$450r + 2,250 = r^2 + 455r$$

Manhattan **GMAT** Prep
the new standard

Typical relationships
among quantities in
RTD charts include the
following: two quantities
equal are the same,
or two quantities sum to
a total.

$$450(r+5) = 450r + r(r+5)$$

$$450r + 2,250 = 450r + r^2 + 5r$$

$$r^2 + 5r - 2,250 = 0$$

Factoring this quadratic is rather challenging. You are looking for two numbers that multiply to 2,250 and differ by 5. The key is to remember that you got 2,250 by multiplying 450 by 5. This product suggests that $45 \times 50 = 2,250$. Moreover, 45 and 50 differ by 5.

$$(r+50)(r-45) = 0$$

$$\rightarrow r = 45 \text{ or } -50$$

−50 miles per hour is not a reasonable rate, so $r = 45$ miles per hour. Liam's actual speed was $r + 5 = 50$ miles per hour.

Average Rate: Don't Just Add and Divide

Consider the following problem:

> If Lucy walks to work at a rate of 4 miles per hour, but she walks home by the same route at a rate of 6 miles per hour, what is Lucy's average walking rate for the round trip?

It is very tempting to find an average rate as you would find any other average: add and divide. Thus, you might say that Lucy's average rate is 5 miles per hour ($4 + 6 = 10$ and $10 \div 2 = 5$). However, this is INCORRECT!

If an object moves the **same distance** twice, but at **different rates**, then *the average rate will NEVER be the average of the two rates given for the two legs of the journey*. In fact, because the object spends more time traveling at the slower rate, *the average rate will be closer to the slower of the two rates than to the faster*.

In order to find the average rate, you must first find the TOTAL combined time for the trips and the TOTAL combined distance for the trips.

First, we need a value for the distance. Since all we need to know to determine the average rate is the *total time* and *total distance*, we can actually pick any number for the distance. The portion of the total distance represented by each part of the trip ("Going" and "Return") will dictate the time.

Pick a Smart Number for the distance. Since 12 is a multiple of the two rates in the problem, 4 and 6, 12 is an ideal choice.

Set up a Multiple RTD Chart:

The times can be found using the *RTD* equation. For the GOING trip, $4t = 12$, so $t = 3$ hrs. For the RETURN trip, $6t = 12$, so $t = 2$ hrs. Thus, the total time is 5 hrs.

	Rate (mi/hr)	×	Time (hr)	=	Distance (mi)
Going	4 mi/hr	×		=	12 mi
Return	6 mi/hr	×		=	12 mi
Total	?	×		=	24 mi

The average rate is NOT the simple average of the two rates in the problem!

Manhattan **GMAT** Prep

Now that we have the total Time and the total Distance, we can find the Average Rate using the RTD formula:

$$RT = D$$
$$r(5) = 24$$
$$r = 4.8 \text{ miles per hour}$$

	Rate (mi/hr)	×	Time (hr)	=	Distance (mi)
Going	4 mi/hr	×	**3 hrs**	=	12 mi
Return	6 mi/hr	×	**2 hrs**	=	12 mi
Total	?	×	**5 hrs**	=	24 mi

Again, 4.8 miles per hour is *not* the simple average of 4 miles per hour and 6 miles per hour. In fact, it is the weighted average of the two rates, with the *times* as the weights.

You can test different numbers for the distance (try 24 or 36) to prove that you will get the same answer, regardless of the number you choose for the distance.

Basic Work Problems

Work problems are just another type of rate problem. Just like all other rate problems, work problems involve three elements: rate, time, and "distance."

WORK: In work problems, distance is replaced by work, which refers to the number of jobs completed or the number of items produced.

TIME: This is the time spent working.

RATE: In motion problems, the rate is a ratio of distance to time, or the amount of distance traveled in one time unit. In work problems, the rate is a ratio of work to time, or the amount of work completed in one time unit.

Figuring Work Rates

Work rates usually include one major twist not seen in distance problems: you often have to *calculate* the work rate.

In distance problems, if the rate (speed) is known, it will normally be *given* to you as a ready-to-use number. In work problems, though, you will usually have to *figure out* the rate from some given information about how many jobs the agent can complete in a given amount of time:

$$\text{Work rate} = \frac{\text{Given \# of jobs}}{\text{Given amount of time}} \text{, or } \frac{1}{\text{Time to complete 1 job}}$$

For instance, if Oscar can perform one hand surgery in 1.5 hours, his work rate is

$$\frac{1 \text{ operation}}{1.5 \text{ hours}} = \frac{2}{3} \text{ operation per hour}$$

Remember the rate is NOT 1.5 hours per hand surgery! Always express work rates as jobs per unit time, not as time per job. Also, you need to be careful to distinguish this type of general information—which is meant to specify the work rate—from the data given about the specific scenario in the problem.

Work problems are just like distance problems, except that the distance traveled is now the work performed.

For example:

> If a copier can make 3 copies every 2 seconds, how long will it take to make 40 copies?

Here, the work is 40 copies, because this is the number of items produced. The time is unknown. The rate is 3 copies/2 seconds, or 1.5 copies per second.

> If it takes Anne 5 hours to paint one fence, and she has been working for 7 hours, how many fences has she painted?

Here the time is 7 hours, because that is the time which Anne spent working. The work done is unknown. Anne's general working rate is 1 fence per 5 hours, or 1/5 fence per hour. Be careful: her rate is not 5 hours per fence, but rather 0.2 fence per hour. Again, always express rates as work per time unit, not time per work unit.

When two or more workers work together on a job, their rates add, not their times. The resulting time will be lower than any individual worker's.

Basic work problems are solved like basic rate problems, using an RTW chart or the RTW equation. Simply replace the distance with the work. They can also be solved with a simple proportion. Here are both methods for Anne's work problem:

RTW CHART   **PROPORTION**

R (fence/hr)	$\times$	T (hr)	$=$	W (fences)
1/5 fence/hr	$\times$	7 hours	$=$	x

$$\frac{5 \text{ hours}}{1 \text{ fence}} = \frac{7 \text{ hours}}{x \text{ fences}}$$

$$RT = W$$

$$\frac{1}{5}(7) = \frac{7}{5}$$

$$5x = 7$$

$$x = \frac{7}{5}$$

Anne has painted 7/5 of a fence, or 1.4 fences. Note that you can set up the proportion either as "hours/fence" or as "fences/hour." You must simply be consistent on both sides of the equation. However, any rate in an $RT = W$ relationship must be in "fences/hour."

Working Together: Add the Rates

The GMAT often presents problems in which several workers working together to complete a job. The trick to these "working together" problems is to determine the combined rate of all the workers working together. This combined working rate is equal to the sum of all the individual working rates. For example, if Machine A can make 5 boxes in an hour, and Machine B can make 12 boxes in an hour, then working together, Machines A and B can make 17 boxes in an hour.

Note that work problems, which are mathematically equivalent to distance problems, feature much less variety than distance problems.

Almost every work problem with multiple people or machines doing work has those people or machines working together. Thus, we can almost always follow this rule: **If two or more agents are performing simultaneous work, add the work rates.**

You can think of "two people working together" as "two people working alongside each other." If Lucas can assemble 1 toy in an hour, and Serena can assemble 2 toys in an hour, then working together, Lucas and Serena can assemble 3 toys in an hour. In other words, Lucas's rate (1 toy per hour) plus Serena's rate (2 toys per hour) equals their joint rate (3 toys per hour).

The only exception to this rule comes in the rare case when one agent's work *undoes* the other agent's work; in that case, you would subtract the rates. For example, one pump might put water *into* a tank, while another pump draws water *out* of that same tank. Again, such problems are very rare.

If work problems involve *time* relations, or relations such as "second-guessing," then the calculations are exactly the same as for the corresponding distance problems (with total work substituted for distance).

> Larry can wash a car in 1 hour, Moe can wash a car in 2 hours, and Curly can wash a car in 4 hours. How long will it take them to wash a car together?

First, find their individual rates, or the amount of work they can do in one hour: Larry's rate is 1 (or 1 car / 1 hour), Moe's rate is 1 car/2 hours, and Curly's rate is 1 car/4 hours. To find their combined rate, sum their individual rates (**not** their times):

$$1 + \frac{1}{2} + \frac{1}{4} = \frac{7}{4} \text{ cars/hr.}$$

Then, create an RTW chart:

R (cars/hr)	×	T (hr)	=	W (cars)
7/4	×	t	=	1

Using the formula $RT = W$, solve for the time:

$$RT = W$$

$$\frac{7}{4}t = 1$$

$$t = \frac{4}{7} \text{ hours, or approximately 34 minutes.}$$

Now consider the following problem.

> Wendy begins sanding a kitchen floor by herself and works for 4 hours. She is then joined by Bruce, and together the two of them finish sanding the floor in 2 hours. If Bruce can sand the floor by himself in 20 hours, how long would it take Wendy to sand the floor by herself?

Always compute any rates in units of work per time, not time per work.

You can attack this problem in different ways. No matter what, though, the first thing you should do is focus on the following piece of information:

> If Bruce can sand the floor by himself in 20 hours...

This specifies the rate at which Bruce works *in general.* Note the use of the word *can* to indicate his general ability. (In the problem scenario, Bruce is *not* sanding the floor by himself.) Bruce's work rate is thus

$$\frac{1 \text{ floor}}{20 \text{ hours}} = \frac{1}{20} \text{ floor/hour}$$

Study the efficient short-cuts in any RTD or RTW solution, to reduce the algebra you need to do on future problems.

You can also write a quick RTW table and solve for his unknown work rate, but if you can learn to write the work rate directly from statements such as *Bruce can sand the floor by himself in 20 hours*, then you will save time. Just make sure that you write the units correctly: work rates should always be work per time, not time per work!

Shortcut Method

As we saw with distance problems, you can lighten your workload by *recasting* and *rephrasing* the problem. In this case, you can perform the following arithmetic steps, using only *one*-row RTW tables at any point. First, focus on the fact that Bruce works alongside Wendy for 2 hours. Since he works at a rate of 1 floor/20 hours, we can set up an RTW chart to figure out how much work Bruce does in those 2 hours:

	R (fl/hr)	×	T (hr)	=	W (fl)
Bruce	1/20	×	2	=	**2/20**

He is therefore able to complete 2/20, or 1/10, of the floor. This means that Wendy has to do 9/10 of the floor in the 6 hours total that she spends working: 4 hours by herself and 2 hours alongside Bruce.

Now we can solve for her work rate, using another RTW chart:

$$\frac{9}{10} \div \frac{6}{1} = \frac{9}{10} \times \frac{1}{6} = \frac{3}{20} \text{ floor/hour}$$

	R (fl/hr)	×	T (hr)	=	W (fl)
Wendy	**3/20**	×	6	=	9/10

Finally, take the reciprocal of her work rate to find the time that it takes Wendy to sand one floor. If she can sand 3/20 of a floor in 1 hour, then she will take 20/3 hours to sand 1 floor. You can also use a final RTW chart to find this time:

$$1 \div \frac{3}{20} = \frac{20}{3} \text{ hours to sand 1 floor}$$

	R (fl/hr)	×	T (hr)	=	W (fl)
Wendy	3/20	×	**20/3**	=	1

Algebraic Method

The problem presents two stages of the work: first, Wendy works by herself, and then she is joined by Bruce. We can set up an RTW chart with two rows to represent these two stages. Optionally, we can add a third row to represent Wendy theoretically sanding one floor by herself. The Ultimate Unknown in the problem is the time that she would take to do so.

The intermediate unknown that we should use is Wendy's refinishing rate, which can be called r. Using the given information (and the work rate we already calculated for Bruce), fill in the chart:

	R (fl/hr)	×	T (hr)	=	W (fl)
Wendy actual	r	×	4	=	
Both actual	$1/20 + r$	×	2	=	
Wendy theoretical	r	×	?	=	1

Now write algebraic expressions in the Work column of the chart:

	R (fl/hr)	×	T (hr)	=	W (fl)
Wendy actual	r	×	4	=	$4r$
Both actual	$1/20 + r$	×	2	=	$2(1/20 + r)$
Wendy theoretical	r	×	?	=	1

Now, the sum of the first two Work expressions is 1, because by the end of those two stages, Wendy and Bruce have sanded exactly 1 floor.

Thus, we can write the equation:

$$4r + 2\left(\frac{1}{20} + r\right) = 1$$

$$4r + \frac{1}{10} + 2r = 1$$

$$6r = \frac{9}{10}$$

$$r = \frac{3}{20}$$

Since the time taken to complete one job is the reciprocal of the rate, Wendy takes 20/3 hours to sand a floor by herself.

Be able to work the problem both ways. Get fast at setting up RTW charts and carrying out the algebra (which generally looks worse than it actually is). At the same time, you should also study the "shortcut" method for any problem and make it your own.

Do not be intimidated by RTD or RTW algebra; it generally looks scarier than it actually is!

Population Problems

The final type of rate problem on the GMAT is the population problem. These can be solved with a population chart. Consider the following example:

> The population of a certain type of bacterium triples every 10 minutes. If the population of a colony 20 minutes ago was 100, in approximately how many minutes from now will the bacteria population reach 24,000?

You can solve simple population problems, such as this one, by using a Population Chart. Make a table with a few rows, labeling one of the middle rows as "NOW". Work forward, backward, or both (as necessary in the problem), obeying any conditions given in the problem statement about the rate of growth or decay.

Time Elapsed	Population
20 minutes ago	100
10 minutes ago	300
NOW	900
in 10 minutes	2,700
in 20 minutes	8,100
in 30 minutes	24,300

For this problem, the Population Chart at right shows that the bacterial population will reach 24,000 about 30 minutes from now.

Use a Population Chart to track the "exponential growth" of populations that double or triple in size over constant intervals of time.

Equations for Exponential Growth or Decay (Advanced)

Most simple, concrete GMAT population problems (with specific numbers) can be solved with Population Charts. A few problems, however, may call for an exponential formula to represent population growth, or they may ask you to interpret such a formula.

Here is how the formula works. Let us imagine that we are told how long it takes to double the population.

> I, or interval, is the amount of time given for the quantity to double.
> S, or starting value, is the size of the population at time zero or "now."
> t, or time, is the variable.

The formula is then written as follows: $\text{Population} = S \cdot 2^{t/I}$

If the population triples in the interval, then we have this variation: $\text{Population} = S \cdot 3^{t/I}$

Likewise, if the population is cut in half in the interval, the formula is $S \cdot (0.5)^{t/I}$

For instance, if a rabbit population currently consists of 2,400 rabbits and doubles every seven months, the rabbit population t months from now will be given by the formula

$$\text{Population} = (2,400) \cdot 2^{t/7}$$

If you know how to write these formulas, you can make short work of any population problem. If the problem asks for a value, you can just plug into the formula, and, of course, if the problem asks for the formula itself, you will be in great shape!

Problem Set

Solve the following problems, using the strategies you have learned in this section. Use RTD or RTW charts as appropriate to organize information.

1. A cat travels at 60 inches/second. How long will it take this cat to travel 300 feet? (12 inches = 1 foot)

2. Water is being poured into a tank at the rate of approximately 4 cubic feet per hour. If the tank is 6 feet long, 4 feet wide, and 8 feet deep, how many hours will it take to fill up the tank?

3. The population of grasshoppers doubles in a particular field every year. Approximately how many years will it take the population to grow from 2,000 grasshoppers to 1,000,000 or more?

4. Two hoses are pouring water into an empty pool. Hose 1 alone would fill up the pool in 6 hours. Hose 2 alone would fill up the pool in 4 hours. How long would it take for both hoses to fill up two-thirds of the pool?

5. One hour after Adrienne started walking the 60 miles from X to Y, James started walking from X to Y as well. Adrienne walks 3 miles per hour, and James walks 1 mile per hour faster than Adrienne. How far from X will James be when he catches up to Adrienne?

    (A) 8 miles (B) 9 miles (C) 10 miles (D) 11 miles (E) 12 miles

6. Machine A produces widgets at a uniform rate of 160 every 40 minutes, and Machine B produces widgets at a uniform rate of 100 every 20 minutes. If the two machines run simultaneously, how long will it take them to produce 207 widgets in total?

7. An empty bucket being filled with paint at a constant rate takes 6 minutes to be filled to 7/10 of its capacity. How much more time will it take to fill the bucket to full capacity?

8. Three workers can fill a tank in 4, 5, or 6 minutes, respectively. How many tanks can be filled by all three workers working together in 2 minutes?

9. 4 years from now, the population of a colony of bees will reach 1.6×10^8. If the population of the colony doubles every 2 years, what was the population 4 years ago?

10. The Technotronic can produce 5 bad songs per hour. Wanting to produce bad songs more quickly, the record label also buys a Wonder Wheel, which works as fast as the Technotronic. Working together, how many bad songs can the two produce in 72 minutes?

11. A car travels from Town A to Town B at an average speed of 40 miles per hour, and returns immediately along the same route at an average speed of 50 miles per hour. What is the average speed in miles per hour for the round-trip?

12. Jack is putting together gift boxes at a rate of 3 per hour in the first hour. Then Jill comes over and yells, "Work faster!" Jack, now nervous, works at the rate of only 2 gift boxes per hour for the next 2 hours. Then Alexandra comes to Jack and whispers, "The steadiest hand is capable of the divine." Jack, calmer, then puts together 5 gift boxes in the fourth hour. What is the average rate at which Jack puts together gift boxes over the entire period?

13. Andrew drove from A to B at 60 miles per hour. Then he realized that he forgot something at A, and drove back at 80 miles per hour. He then zipped back to B at 90 mph. What was his approximate average speed in miles per hour for the entire night?

14. A bullet train leaves Kyoto for Tokyo traveling 240 miles per hour at 12 noon. Ten minutes later, a train leaves Tokyo for Kyoto traveling 160 miles per hour. If Tokyo and Kyoto are 300 miles apart, at what time will the trains pass each other?

(A)12:40 pm (B) 12:49 pm (C) 12:55 pm (D) 1:00 pm (E) 1:05 pm

15. Nicky and Cristina are running a 1,000 meter race. Since Cristina is faster than Nicky, she gives him a 12 second head start. If Cristina runs at a pace of 5 meters per second and Nicky runs at a pace of only 3 meters per second, how many seconds will Nicky have run before Cristina catches up to him?

(A) 15 seconds (B) 18 seconds (C) 25 seconds (D) 30 seconds (E) 45 seconds

16. Victor's job requires him to complete a series of identical jobs. If Victor is supervised at work, he finishes each job three days faster than if he is unsupervised. If Victor works for 144 days and is supervised for half the time, he will finish a total of 36 jobs. How long would it take Victor to complete 10 jobs without any supervision?

1. **1 minute:** This is a simple application of the $RT = D$ formula, involving one unit conversion. First convert the rate, 60 inches/second, into 5 feet/second (given that 12 inches = 1 foot). Substitute this value for R. Substitute the distance, 300 feet, for D. Then solve:

$(5 \text{ ft/s})(t) = 300 \text{ ft}$

$t = \dfrac{300 \text{ ft}}{5 \text{ ft/s}} = 60 \text{ seconds} = 1 \text{ minute}$

R (ft/sec)	×	T (sec)	=	D (ft)
5	×	t	=	300

2. **48 hours:** The capacity of the tank is $6 \times 4 \times 8$, or 192 cubic feet. Use the $RT = W$ equation, substituting the rate, 4 ft³/hour, for R, and the capacity, 192 cubic feet, for W.

R (ft³/hr)	×	T (hr)	=	W (ft³)
4	×	t	=	192

$(4 \text{ cubic feet/hr})(t) = 192 \text{ cubic feet}$

$t = \dfrac{192 \text{ cubic feet}}{4 \text{ cubic feet/hr}} = 48 \text{ hours}$

3. **9 years:** Organize the information given in a population chart. Notice that since the population is increasing exponentially, it does not take very long for the population to top 1,000,000.

Time Elapsed	Population
NOW	2,000
1 year	4,000
2 years	8,000
3 years	16,000
4 years	32,000
5 years	64,000
6 years	128,000
7 years	256,000
8 years	512,000
9 years	1,024,000

4. $1\dfrac{3}{5}$ **hours :** If Hose 1 can fill the pool in 6 hours, its rate is 1/6 "pool per hour," or the fraction of the job it can do in one hour. Likewise, if Hose 2 can fill the pool in 4 hours, its rate is 1/4 pool per hour. Therefore, the combined rate is 5/12 pool per hour (1/4 + 1/6 = 5/12).

$RT = W$
$(5/12)t = 2/3$

$t = \left(\dfrac{2}{3}\right)\left(\dfrac{12}{5}\right) = \dfrac{8}{5} = 1\dfrac{3}{5} \text{ hours}$

R (pool/hr)	×	T (hr)	=	W (pool)
5/12	×	t	=	2/3

*Manhattan*GMAT*Prep
the new standard

5. 12 miles: Organize this information in an RTD chart as follows.

Set up algebraic equations to relate the information in the chart, using the $RT = D$ equation.

	R (mi/hr)	×	T (hr)	=	D (mi)
Adrienne	3	×	$t+1$	=	d
James	4	×	t	=	d
Total	—				$2d$

ADRIENNE: $3(t + 1) = d$
JAMES: $4t = d$

Substitute $4t$ for d in the first equation:

$$3(t + 1) = 4t$$
$$3t + 3 = 4t$$
$$t = 3 \quad \text{Therefore, } d = 4(3) = 12 \text{ miles.}$$

Alternatively, you can model this problem as a "Chase." Adrienne has a 3-mile headstart on James (since Adrienne started walking 1 hour before James, and Adrienne's speed is 3 miles per hour). Since James is walking 1 mile per hour faster than Adrienne, it will take 3 hours for him to catch up to Adrienne. Therefore, he will have walked (4 miles per hour)(3 hours) = 12 miles by the time he catches up to Adrienne.

6. 23 minutes: Machine A produces 160 widgets every 40 minutes; therefore, it produces 4 widgets every minute. Machine B produces 100 widgets every 20 minutes, or 5 widgets a minute. Together the two machines will produce 4 + 5 = 9 widgets per minute. Substitute this rate into the $RT = W$ equation, using the target work of 207 widgets for W:

	R (wid/min)	×	T (min)	=	W (wid)
	9	×	t	=	207

(9 widgets/min) t = 207 widgets
$t = 207 \div 9 = 23$ minutes

7. $2\dfrac{4}{7}$ minutes: Use the $RT = W$ equation to solve for the rate, with $t = 6$ minutes and $w = 7/10$.

	R (bkt/min)	×	T (min)	=	W (bucket)
	r	×	6	=	7/10

$r(6 \text{ minutes}) = 7/10$

$r = 7/10 \div 6 = \dfrac{7}{60}$ buckets per minute.

Then, substitute this rate into the equation again, using 3/10 for w (the remaining work to be done).

	R (bkt/min)	×	T (min)	=	W (bucket)
	7/60	×	t	=	3/10

$$\left(\frac{7}{60}\right)t = \frac{3}{10}$$

$$t = \frac{3}{10} \div \frac{7}{60} = \frac{18}{7} = 2\frac{4}{7} \text{ minutes}$$

8. $1\frac{7}{30}$ **tanks:** Since this is a "working together" problem, add the individual rates.

Remember that the rates need to be in tanks per minute, so we need to take the reciprocal of the given "minutes per tank":

$$\frac{1}{a} + \frac{1}{b} + \frac{1}{c} = \frac{1}{x}$$

$$\frac{1}{4} + \frac{1}{5} + \frac{1}{6} = \frac{1}{x}$$

	R (tank/min)	×	T (min)	=	W (tanks)
Worker 1	1/4	×	4	=	1
Worker 2	1/5	×	5	=	1
Worker 3	1/6	×	6	=	1
Total	1/4 + 1/5 + 1/6				1

Remember to find a common denominator:

$$\frac{15}{60} + \frac{12}{60} + \frac{10}{60} = \frac{37}{60}$$

The 3 workers have a combined rate of 37/60 tanks per minute. Use the $RT = W$ equation to find the total work that can be done in 2 minutes:

$$\left(\frac{37}{60}\right)(2 \text{ minutes}) = \frac{37}{30} = 1\frac{7}{30} \text{ tanks.}$$

9. 1×10^7: Organize the information given in a population chart.

Then, convert:
$0.1 \times 10^8 = 10,000,000 = 1 \times 10^7$ bees.

Time Elapsed	Population
4 years ago	0.1×10^8
2 years ago	0.2×10^8
NOW	0.4×10^8
in 2 years	0.8×10^8
in 4 years	1.6×10^8

10. **12 songs:** Since this is a "working together" problem, add the individual rates: 5 + 5 = 10 songs per hour.

The two machines together can produce 10 bad songs in 1 hour. Convert the given time into hours:

$$\left(72 \text{ minutes}\right)\left(\frac{1 \text{ hour}}{60 \text{ minutes}}\right) = \frac{72}{60} = 1.2 \text{ hours}$$

Then, use the $RT = W$ equation to find the total work done:

$$(10)(1.2 \text{ hours}) = w$$
$$w = 12 \text{ bad songs}$$

	R (songs/hr)	×	T (hr)	=	W (songs)
	10	×	1.2	=	w

11. $44\frac{4}{9}$ **miles per hour :** Use a Multiple RTD chart to solve this problem. Start by selecting a Smart Number for d: 200 miles. (This is a common multiple of the 2 rates in the problem.) Then, work backwards to find the time for each trip and the total time:

	R (mi/hr)	×	T (hr)	=	D (mi)
A to B	40	×	t_1	=	200
B to A	50	×	t_2	=	200
Total	—		t		400

$$t_1 = \frac{200}{40} = 5 \text{ hrs} \qquad t_2 = \frac{200}{50} = 4 \text{ hrs} \qquad t = 4 + 5 = 9 \text{ hours}$$

The average speed $= \dfrac{\text{total distance}}{\text{total time}} = \dfrac{400}{9} = 44\frac{4}{9}$ miles per hour.

Do NOT simply average 40 miles per hour and 50 miles per hour to get 45 miles per hour. The fact that the right answer is very close to this wrong result makes this error especially pernicious: avoid it at all costs!

12. **3 boxes per hour:** The average rate is equal to the total work done divided by the time in which the work was done. Remember that you cannot simply average the rates. You must find the total work and total time. The total time is 4 hours. To find the total work, add up the boxes Jack put together in each hour: $3 + 2 + 2 + 5 = 12$. Therefore, the average rate is $\dfrac{12}{4}$, or 3 boxes per hour.

13. **Approximately 74.5 mph:** Use a Multiple RTD chart to solve this problem. Start by selecting a Smart Number for d: 720 miles. (This is a common multiple of the 3 rates in the problem.) Then, work backwards to find the time for each trip and the total time:

	R (mi/hr)	×	T (hr)	=	D (mi)
A to B	60	×	t_A	=	720
B to A	80	×	t_B	=	720
A to B	90	×	t_C	=	720
Total	—		t		2,160

$$t_A = \frac{720}{60} = 12 \text{ hrs}$$

$$t_B = \frac{720}{80} = 9 \text{ hrs}$$

$$t_C = \frac{720}{90} = 8 \text{ hrs}$$

$$t = 12 + 9 + 8 = 29 \text{ hours}$$

The average speed $= \dfrac{\text{total distance}}{\text{total time}} = \dfrac{2,160}{29} \cong 74.5$ miles per hour

14. **12:49 P.M.:** This is a "Kiss" problem in which the trains are moving TOWARDS each other.

Solve this problem by filling in the RTD chart. Note that the train going from Kyoto to Tokyo leaves first, so its time is longer by 10 minutes, which is 1/6 hour.

	R (mi/hr)	×	T (hr)	=	D (mi)
Train K to T	240	×	t + 1/6	=	240(t + 1/6)
Train T to K	160	×	t	=	160t
Total	—		—		300

Next, write the expressions for the distance that each train travels, in terms of t. Now, sum those distances and set that total equal to 300 miles.

$$240\left(t+\frac{1}{6}\right)+160t = 300$$
$$240t + 40 + 160t = 300$$
$$400t = 260$$
$$20t = 13$$
$$t = \frac{13}{20}\,\text{hour} = \frac{39}{60}\,\text{hour} = 39\,\text{minutes}$$

The first train leaves at 12 noon. The second train leaves at 12:10 P.M. Thirty-nine minutes after the second train has left, at 12:49 P.M., the trains pass each other.

15. **30 seconds:** This is a "Chase" problem in which the people are moving in the SAME DIRECTION.

Fill in the RTD chart. Note that Nicky starts 12 seconds before Cristina, so Nicky's time is $t + 12$.

	R (m/s)	×	T (second)	=	D (meter)
Cristina	5	×	t	=	5t
Nicky	3	×	t + 12	=	3(t + 12)

Write expressions for the total distance, and then set these two distances equal to each other.

CRISTINA: $5t$ = distance   NICKY: $3(t + 12)$ = distance

COMBINE: $5t = 3(t + 12)$
$5t = 3t + 36$
$2t = 36$
$t = 18$

Therefore, Nicky will have run for $18 + 12 = 30$ seconds before Cristina catches up to him.

16. **60 days:** The unknowns in this problem are *rates*: namely, Victor's work rates in each of the two situations (supervised and unsupervised). Since there is no easy relationship between the rates themselves, you should not designate the rates directly with variables. Instead, you should turn to the stated relationship between Victor's supervised and unsupervised *times* to complete a job: he can complete one job in t days if he is unsupervised, and one job in $(t - 3)$ days if he is supervised. (You could also call these quantities $t + 3$ and t, respectively, but the first approach is better because t then relates more directly to the quantity you are actually interested in at the end of the problem.) Therefore, Victor's work rates are as follows:

Victor works at a rate of $\dfrac{1 \text{ job}}{t \text{ days}} = \dfrac{1}{t}$ job/day (supervised) and $\dfrac{1 \text{ job}}{(t-3) \text{ days}} = \dfrac{1}{t-3}$ job/day (unsupervised).

Set up a RTW chart:

	Rate (job/day)	×	Time (days)	=	Total Work (jobs)
Supervised	$\dfrac{1}{t-3}$	×	72	=	$\dfrac{72}{t-3}$
Unsupervised	$\dfrac{1}{t}$	×	72	=	$\dfrac{72}{t}$
Total	—	×	[144]	=	36

In this case, the rates *do not* add, because the supervised and unsupervised work are not done simultaneously. You could technically add the two times, but you have no reason to do so (as the problem does not ask you to calculate anything requiring such a calculation, such as the average work rate for all 144 days). The "total work" entries do add, yielding the equation

$$\frac{72}{t-3} + \frac{72}{t} = 36$$

First, divide through by the common denominator $t(t-3)$:

$$\frac{2}{t-3} + \frac{2}{t} = 1$$

Now, multiply through by the common denominator $t(t-3)$:

$$2t + 2(t-3) = t(t-3)$$
$$2t + 2t - 6 = t^2 - 3t$$
$$0 = t^2 - 7t + 6$$
$$0 = (t-1)(t-6)$$
$$t = 1 \text{ day or } t = 6 \text{ days}$$

The first solution ($t = 1$ day) is nonsensical, because it would make the quantity $t - 3$ (the duration of a supervised job) negative. Therefore, Victor takes 6 days to complete a job with no supervision. To complete ten such jobs, then, he needs 60 days.

*Manhattan*GMAT Prep
the new standard

Chapter 3
of
WORD TRANSLATIONS

RATIOS

In This Chapter . . .

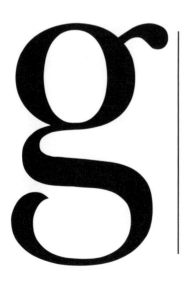

- Labeling Ratios
- Proportions
- The Unknown Multiplier
- Multiple Ratios: Make a Common Term

RATIOS

A ratio expresses a particular relationship between two or more quantities.

<u>Some ratios express a relationship between quantities with the same units:</u>

> The two partners spend time working in the ratio of 1 to 3. For every 1 hour the first partner works, the second partner works 3 hours.

> Three sisters invest in a certain stock in the ratio of 2 to 3 to 8. For every $2 the first sister invests, the second sister invests $3, and the third sister invests $8.

<u>Other ratios express a relationship between different quantities:</u>

> The ratio of men to women in the room is 3 to 4. For every 3 men, there are 4 women.

> The crate is filled with apples, oranges, and peaches in the ratio of 1 to 4 to 5. For every 1 apple, there are 4 oranges and 5 peaches.

<u>All ratios can be expressed in different ways:</u>

> (1) Using the word "to," as in 3 to 4
> (2) Using a colon, as in 3 : 4
>
> (3) By writing a fraction, as in $\dfrac{3}{4}$ (only for ratios of 2 quantities)

<u>Ratios can express a part-part relationship or a part-whole relationship:</u>

> A part–part relationship: The ratio of men to women in the office is 3:4.
> A part–whole relationship: There are 3 men for every 7 employees.

<u>The relationship that ratios express is division:</u>

> If the ratio of men to women in the office is 3 : 4, then the number of men *divided*
>
> *by* the number of women equals $\dfrac{3}{4}$, or 0.75.

It is very important to remember that ratios only express a *relationship* between two or more items; they do not provide enough information, on their own, to determine the exact quantity for each item. For example, knowing that the ratio of men to women in an office is 3 to 4 does NOT tell us exactly how many men and how many women are in the office. All we

know is that the number of men is $\dfrac{3}{4}$ the number of women.

Ratios express a
part–part or a
part–whole relationship.

Label Each Part of the Ratio with Units

The order in which a ratio is given is vital. For example, "the ratio of dogs to cats is 2 : 3" is very different from "the ratio of dogs to cats is 3 : 2." The first ratio says that for every 2 dogs, there are 3 cats. The second ratio says that for every 3 dogs, there are 2 cats.

It is very easy to accidentally reverse the order of a ratio—especially on a timed test like the GMAT. Therefore, to avoid these reversals, always write units on either the ratio itself or the variables you create, or both.

Thus, if the ratio of dogs to cats is 2 : 3, you can write $\dfrac{x \text{ dogs}}{y \text{ cats}} = \dfrac{2 \text{ dogs}}{3 \text{ cats}}$, or simply

$\dfrac{x \text{ dogs}}{y \text{ cats}} = \dfrac{2}{3}$, or even $\dfrac{D}{C} = \dfrac{2 \text{ dogs}}{3 \text{ cats}}$, where D and C are variables standing for the number of dogs and cats, respectively.

Solve simple ratio problems with proportions.

However, do not just write $\dfrac{x}{y} = \dfrac{2}{3}$. You could easily forget which variable stands for cats and which for dogs.

Also, NEVER write $\dfrac{2d}{3c}$. The reason is that you might think that d and c stand for *variables*—that is, numbers in their own right. Always write the full unit out.

Proportions

Simple ratio problems can be solved with a proportion.

> The ratio of girls to boys in the class is 4 to 7. If there are 35 boys in the class, how many girls are there?

Step 1: Set up a labeled PROPORTION:

$$\frac{4 \text{ girls}}{7 \text{ boys}} = \frac{x \text{ girls}}{35 \text{ boys}}$$

Step 2: Cross-multiply to solve:

$$140 = 7x$$
$$x = 20$$

To save time, you should cancel factors out of proportions before cross-multiplying. You can cancel factors either vertically within a fraction or horizontally across an equals sign:

$$\frac{4 \text{ girls}}{7 \text{ boys}} = \frac{x \text{ girls}}{35 \text{ boys}} \qquad \frac{4 \text{ girls}}{\cancel{7} \text{ 1 boy}} = \frac{x \text{ girls}}{\cancel{35} \text{ 5 boys}} \qquad x = 20$$

Never cancel factors diagonally across an equals sign. Always cross-multiply.

The Unknown Multiplier

For more complicated ratio problems, it is helpful to make use of the "Unknown Multiplier" technique.

> The ratio of men to women in a room is 3 : 4. If there are 56 people in the room, how many of the people are men?

Using the methods from the previous page, you can write the ratio relationship as $\frac{M \text{ men}}{W \text{ women}} = \frac{3}{4}$. Together with $M + W = \text{Total} = 56$, you can solve for M (and W, for that matter). The algebra for these "two equations and two unknowns" is not too difficult.

However, there is even an easier way. It requires a slight shift in your thinking, but if you can make this shift, you can save yourself a lot of work on some problems. Instead of representing the number of men as M, represent it as $3x$, where x is some unknown (positive) number. Likewise, instead of representing the number of women as W, represent it as $4x$, where x is the same unknown number.

What does this seemingly odd step accomplish? It guarantees that the ratio of men to women is 3 : 4. The ratio of men to women can now be expressed as $\frac{3x}{4x}$, which reduces to $\frac{3}{4}$, the desired ratio. (Note that we can cancel the x's because we ensure that x is not zero.) This variable x is known as the Unknown Multiplier. The Unknown Multiplier allows us to reduce the number of variables, making the algebra easier.

Now determine the value of the Unknown Multiplier, using the other equation.

$$\text{Men} + \text{Women} = \text{Total} = 56$$
$$3x + 4x = 56$$
$$7x = 56$$
$$x = 8$$

Now we know that the value of x, the Unknown Multiplier, is 8. Therefore, we can determine the exact number of men and women in the room:

The number of men = $3x = 3(8) = 24$. The number of women = $4x = 4(8) = 32$.

When *can* you use the Unknown Multiplier? You can use it ONCE per problem. Every other ratio in the problem must be set up with a proportion. You should never have two Unknown Multipliers in the same problem.

When *should* you use the Unknown Multiplier? You should use it when neither quantity in the ratio is already equal to a number or a variable expression. Generally, the first ratio in a problem can be set up with an Unknown Multiplier. In the "girls & boys" problem on the previous page, however, we can glance ahead and see that the number of boys is given as 35. This means that we can just set up a simple proportion to solve the problem.

For more complicated ratio problems, use the Unknown Multiplier.

The Unknown Multiplier is particularly useful with three-part ratios, as we see in the next problem:

> A recipe calls for amounts of lemon juice, wine, and water in the ratio of 2 : 5 : 7. If all three combined yield 35 milliliters of liquid, how much wine was included?

Make a quick table:

Lemon Juice	Wine	Water	Total
2x	5x	7x	14x

Now solve: $14x = 35$, or $x = 2.5$. Thus, the amount of wine is $5x = 5(2.5) = 12.5$ milliliters.

In this problem, the Unknown Multiplier turns out not to be an integer. This result is perfectly fine, because the problem deals with continuous, uncountable quantities (milliliters of liquids). In problems like the first one, which deals with countable quantities (men and women), the Unknown Multiplier must be a positive integer; in this case the multiplier is literally the number of "complete sets" of 3 men and 4 women each.

> To combine ratios with a common element, multiply each ratio to make a common term.

Multiple Ratios: Make a Common Term

You may encounter two ratios containing a common element. To combine the ratios, you can use a process remarkably similar to creating a common denominator for fractions.

Because ratios act like fractions, you can multiply both sides of a ratio (or all sides, if there are more than two) by the same number, just as you can multiply the numerator and denominator of a fraction by the same number. You can change *fractions* to have common *denominators*. Likewise, you can change *ratios* to have common *terms* corresponding to the same quantity. Consider the following problem:

> In a box containing action figures of the three Fates from Greek mythology, there are three figures of Clotho for every two figures of Atropos, and five figures of Clotho for every four figures of Lachesis.
> (a)   What is the least number of action figures that could be in the box?
> (b)   What is the ratio of Lachesis figures to Atropos figures?

(a) In symbols, this problem tells you that $C : A = 3 : 2$ and $C : L = 5 : 4$. Right now, you cannot combine these ratios into a single ratio of all three quantities, because the terms for *C* are different. However, you can fix that problem with multiplication by the right numbers, making both *C*'s into the *least common multiple* of the current values.

Multiply the 3 : 2 ratio by 5 (both "top" and "bottom"), and you get $C : A = 15 : 10$.

Likewise, multiply the 5 : 4 ratio by 3 to get $C : L = 15 : 12$. Now that you have the same number for *C* in both ratios, you can simply combine the ratios: $C : L : A = 15 : 12 : 10$. The actual *numbers* of action figures are these three numbers times an Unknown Multiplier, which must be a positive integer. Using the smallest possible multiplier, 1, there are $15 + 12 + 10 = 37$ action figures.

(b) Once you have combined the ratios, you can extract the numbers corresponding to the quantities in question and disregard the others: $L : A = 12 : 10$, which reduces to 6 : 5.

Problem Set

Solve the following problems, using the strategies you have learned in this section. Use proportions and the unknown multiplier to organize ratios.

For problems 1 through 5, assume that neither x nor y is equal to 0, to permit division by x and by y.

1.   48 : 2x is equivalent to 144 : 600. What is x?

2. x : 15 is equivalent to y to x. Given that $y = 3x$, what is x?

3.   2x : y is equivalent to 4x : 8500. What is y?

4.   8 : x^2 is equivalent to 56 : 252. What is x?

5.   90 : x is equivalent to 3x^2 : x^2. What is x?

6.   Brian's marbles have a red to yellow ratio of 2 : 1. If Brian has 22 red marbles, how many yellow marbles does Brian have?

7.   Initially, the men and women in a room were in the ratio of 5 : 7. Six women leave the room. If there are 35 men in the room, how many women are left in the room?

8.   Initially, the men and women in a room were in the ratio of 4 : 5. Then, 2 men entered the room and 3 women left the room. Then, the number of women doubled. Now there are 14 men in the room. How many women are currently in the room?

9.   It is currently raining cats and dogs in the ratio of 5 : 6. If there are 18 fewer cats than dogs, how many dogs are raining?

10.   The amount of time that three people worked on a special project was in the ratio of 2 to 3 to 5. If the project took 110 hours, how many more hours did the hardest working person work than the person who worked the least?

11.   Alexandra needs to mix cleaning solution in the following ratio: 1 part bleach for every 4 parts water. When mixing the solution, Alexandra makes a mistake and mixes in half as much bleach as she ought to have. The total solution consists of 27 mL. How much bleach did Alexandra put into the solution?

12. Initially, there are 32 people in a room, with a ratio of 5 men for every 3 women. 18 men leave, and the number of women in the room then diminishes, so that the number of women in the room is equal to twice the number of men in the room. In order to have a 2 : 1 ratio of men to women in the room, how many more men must be added?

13. 3 machines have a productivity ratio of 1 to 2 to 5. All 3 machines are working on a job for 3 hours. At the beginning of the 4th hour, the slowest machine breaks. It is fixed at the beginning of hour seven, and begins working again. The job is done in nine hours. What was the ratio of the work performed by the fastest machine to the work performed by the slowest?

14. It takes the average dryer 80 minutes to dry one full load of Bob's laundry. Bob has one average dryer, and also decides to try one "Super Jumbo-Tron Dryer-Matic", which is faster than the average dryer by a ratio of 5 : 4. Bob has three loads of laundry, and both machines are so precise that he can set them to the minute. How many minutes does it take for him to dry his three loads? (Assume that no time passes between loads and that he can use both machines concurrently. Assume also that he never runs a machine with less than a full load. Finally, assume that Bob does not partially dry a load in one machine and then switch it to the other.)

15. 4 sewing machines can sew shirts in the ratio 1 : 2 : 3 : 5. The fastest can sew a shirt in 2 hours. However, the fastest machine breaks. How long will it take the other three machines to sew a total of 3 shirts?

1. **100:**

$$\frac{48}{2x} = \frac{144}{600}$$

Simplify the ratios and cancel factors horizontally across the equals sign.

$$\frac{\cancel{24}\,4}{x} = \frac{\cancel{6}\,1}{25}$$

Then, cross-multiply: $x = 100$.

2. **45:**

$$\frac{x}{15} = \frac{y}{x}$$

First, substitute $3x$ for y.

$$\frac{x}{15} = \frac{3x}{x} = 3$$

Then, solve for x: $x = 3 \times 15 = 45$.

3. **4,250:**

$$\frac{2x}{y} = \frac{4x}{8,500}$$

First, simplify the ratio on the right-hand side of the equation.

$$\frac{2x}{y} = \frac{x}{2,125}$$

Then, cross-multiply: $4,250x = xy$.
Divide both sides of the equation by x: $y = 4,250$.

4. **{−6, 6}:**

$$\frac{\cancel{8}\,1}{x^2} = \frac{\cancel{56}\,7}{252} = \frac{1}{36}$$

Simplify the right-hand ratio and cancel factors horizontally.

Then, cross-multiply: $x^2 = 36$.
Find the square root of both sides: $x = \{-6, 6\}$.

5. **30:**

$$\frac{90}{x} = \frac{3x^2}{x^2}$$

First, simplify the ratio on the right-hand side of the equation.

$$\frac{90}{x} = 3$$

Then, solve for x: $3x = 90$
$x = 30$

6. **11:** Write a proportion to solve this problem: $\dfrac{\text{red}}{\text{yellow}} = \dfrac{2}{1} = \dfrac{22}{x}$

Cross-multiply to solve: $2x = 22$
$x = 11$

7. **43:** First, establish the starting number of men and women with a proportion, and simplify.

$$\frac{5 \text{ men}}{7 \text{ women}} = \frac{35 \text{ men}}{x \text{ women}} \qquad \frac{\cancel{5}\;1 \text{ man}}{7 \text{ women}} = \frac{\cancel{35}\;7 \text{ men}}{x \text{ women}}$$

Cross-multiply: $x = 49$.

If 6 women leave the room, there are $49 - 6 = 43$ women left.

8. **24:** Use the Unknown Multiplier to solve this problem. Initially, there are $4x$ men in the room and $5x$ women. Then, follow the series of entrances and exits one-by-one to establish the number of men and women who are currently in the room, in terms of x.

	Before	After	Finally
Men	$4x$	$4x + 2$	$4x + 2$
Women	$5x$	$5x - 3$	$2(5x - 3)$

Men: $4x + 2 = 14$ *The unknown multiplier is 3.* Women: $2(5x - 3) = ?$
$4x = 12$ *Plug 3 in for x.* $\longrightarrow$ $2[5(3) - 3] = 2(12) = 24$
$x = 3$

9. **108:** If the ratio of cats to dogs is 5 : 6, then there are $5x$ cats and $6x$ dogs (using the Unknown Multiplier). Express the fact that there are 18 fewer cats than dogs with an equation:

$$5x + 18 = 6x$$
$$x = 18$$

Therefore, there are $6(18) = 108$ dogs.

10. **33 hours:** Use an equation with the Unknown Multiplier to represent the total hours put in by the three people:

$$2x + 3x + 5x = 110$$
$$10x = 110$$
$$x = 11$$

Therefore, the hardest working person put in $5(11) = 55$ hours, and the person who worked the least put in $2(11) = 22$ hours. This represents a difference of $55 - 22 = 33$ hours.

11. **3 parts:** The correct ratio is 1 : 4, which means that there should be x parts bleach and $4x$ parts water. However, Alexandra put in half as much bleach as she should have, so she put in $\dfrac{x}{2}$ parts bleach. You can represent this with an equation: $\dfrac{x}{2} + 4x = 27$.

$x + 8x = 54$ The Unknown Multiplier is 6.
$9x = 54$ Therefore, Alexandra put $6 \div 2$, or
$x = 6$ 3 parts bleach into the solution.

*Manhattan*GMAT*Prep*
the new standard

12. **6:** First, use the Unknown Multiplier to find the total number of men and women in the room. The number of men is $5x$. The number of women is $3x$. If there are 32 people in the room, then:

$$5x + 3x = 32$$
$$8x = 32 \qquad \text{Initially, there are } 5(4) = 20 \text{ men and } 3(4) = 12 \text{ women in the room.}$$
$$x = 4$$

Then, 18 men leave, and there are 2 men and 12 women in the room. Finally, enough women leave so that there are twice as many women in the room as there are men. Since we know there are 2 men in the room, there must be only 4 women left. In order to have a men to women ratio of 2 : 1, there must be 8 men in the room, so 6 men must be added.

13. **15 to 2:** Machine A can produce x jobs in one hour; its rate of production is x. Machine B can produce $2x$ jobs in one hour; its rate of production is $2x$. Machine C can produce $5x$ jobs in one hour; its rate of production is $5x$. Machine C, the fastest machine, worked for 9 hours; use the $RT = W$ equation to calculate the work done: $5x(9) = 45x$. Machine A, the slowest machine, worked for 6 hours; use the $RT = W$ equation to calculate the work done: $x(6) = 6x$. The ratio of the work done by C to the work done by A is therefore 45 to 6, or 15 to 2.

14. **128 minutes:** The super dryer is faster than the average dryer by a ratio of 5 : 4. It takes the average dryer 80 minutes to dry a load; therefore, its rate is 1/80 of a load in a minute. Use a proportion to find the rate of the super dryer:

$$\frac{5}{4} = \frac{x}{1/80} \qquad \text{Cross-multiply: } 5\left(\frac{1}{80}\right) = 4x \qquad x = \frac{1}{64}$$

It takes the super dryer 64 minutes to dry a load.

Assume that two of the three loads will be dried by the super dryer. This will take $2(64) = 128$ minutes. During those 128 minutes, the third load will be dried by the average dryer. However, since this is happening simultaneously, we do not need to add these 80 minutes.

Incidentally, if Bob is allowed to switch partially-dried loads between dryers, he can beat this time of 128 minutes. Under the current scheme, the average dryer is idle for 48 minutes, after it dries the third load. By partially drying loads (4/9 of the way in the regular dryer, which is slower, and the remaining 5/9 of the way in the super dryer) and switching loads, Bob can keep both dryers running at capacity all the time and finish the full job in 320/3 minutes, which is just under 107 minutes. The concept is to have the faster dryer do an exact portion more of the work, according to the ratio of rates. Since this dryer is 5/4 faster, it should do 5 units of work for every 4 units of work the regular dryer does. In this way, the dryers take exactly the same amount of time to do their allotted work. Neither dryer is ever idle, resulting in the quickest time to complete all the drying.

15. **5 hours:** The first sewing machine can sew $1x$ shirts, the second can sew $2x$ shirts, the third $3x$ shirts, and the fastest machine $5x$ shirts. If the fastest machine can sew a shirt in 2 hours, its rate is 1/2 shirts/hr. We can use the rate of the fastest machine to solve for the Unknown Multiplier, x.

$$5x = \frac{1}{2}$$

$$x = \frac{1}{10}$$

However, recall that this machine is broken. To find the rates of the other machines, use the Unknown Multiplier x, which we now know is equal to one-tenth.

Machine 1: $1x = 1\left(\dfrac{1}{10}\right) = \dfrac{1}{10}$

Machine 2: $2x = 2\left(\dfrac{1}{10}\right) = \dfrac{2}{10}$

Machine 3: $3x = 3\left(\dfrac{1}{10}\right) = \dfrac{3}{10}$

Since this is a "working together" problem, add the individual rates: $\dfrac{1}{10} + \dfrac{2}{10} + \dfrac{3}{10} = \dfrac{6}{10}$

Together, Machines 1–3 can make 6/10 shirts in one hour. To find out how long it will take them to make 3 shirts, use the $RT = W$ equation:

(6/10 shirts/hr)t = 3 shirts

$t = 3 \div \dfrac{6}{10} = 5$ hours

	R	×	T	=	W
	(s/hr)		(hr)		(shirts)
	6/10	×	t	=	3

Chapter 4
of
WORD TRANSLATIONS

COMBINATORICS

In This Chapter . . .

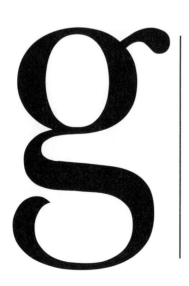

- The Fundamental Counting Principle
- Simple Factorials
- Anagrams
- Combinatorics with Repitition: Anagram Grids
- Multiple Arrangements
- Arrangements with Constraints
- Combination and Permutation Formulas (Advanced)
- Disguised Combinatorics (Advanced)

COMBINATORICS

Many GMAT problems are, ultimately, just about counting things. Although counting may seem to be a simple concept, counting *problems* can be complex. In fact, counting problems have given rise to a whole sub-field of mathematics: *combinatorics*, which is essentially "advanced counting." This chapter presents the fundamentals of combinatorics that are essential on the GMAT.

In combinatorics, we are often counting the **number of possibilities**: how many different ways you can arrange things. For instance, we might ask the following:

(1)   A restaurant menu features five appetizers, six entrées, and three desserts. If a dinner special consists of one appetizer, one entrée, and one dessert, how many different dinner specials are possible?

(2)   Four people sit down in 4 fixed chairs lined up in a row. How many different seating arrangements are possible?

(3)   If there are 7 people in a room, but only 3 chairs in a row, how many different seating arrangements are possible?

(4)   If a group of 3 people is to be chosen from 7 people in a room, how many different groups are possible?

> To count all your options, multiply the choices you have for each separate option.

The Fundamental Counting Principle

Counting problems commonly feature multiple separate choices. Whether such choices are made simultaneously (e.g., choosing types of bread and filling for a sandwich) or sequentially (e.g., choosing among routes between successive towns on a road trip), the rule for combining the numbers of options is the same.

Fundamental Counting Principle: If you must make a number of separate decisions, then MULTIPLY the numbers of ways to make each *individual* decision to find the number of ways to make *all* the decisions.

To grasp this principle intuitively, imagine that you are making a simple sandwich. You will choose ONE type of bread out of 2 types (Rye or Whole wheat) and ONE type of filling out of 3 types (Chicken salad, Peanut butter, or Tuna fish). How many different kinds of sandwich can you make? Well, you can always list all the possibilities:

Rye – Chicken salad   Whole wheat – Chicken salad
Rye – Peanut butter   Whole wheat – Peanut butter
Rye – Tuna fish   Whole wheat – Tuna fish

We see that there are 6 possible sandwiches overall in this table. Instead of listing all the sandwiches, you can simply **multiply** the number of bread choices (the columns) by the number of filling choices (the rows), as dictated by the Fundamental Counting Principle:
2 breads × 3 fillings = 6 possible sandwiches.

As its name implies, the Fundamental Counting Principle is essential to solving combinatorics problems. It is the basis of many other techniques that appear later in this chapter. You can also use the Fundamental Counting Principle directly.

> A restaurant menu features five appetizers, six entrées, and three desserts. If a dinner special consists of one appetizer, one entrée, and one dessert, how many different dinner specials are possible?

This problem features three decisions: an appetizer (which can be chosen in 5 different ways), an entrée (6 ways), and a dessert (3 ways). Since the choices are separate, the total number of dinner specials is the product $5 \times 6 \times 3 = 90$.

In theory, you could *list* all 90 dinner specials. In practice, that is the last thing you would ever want to do! It would take far too long, and it is likely that you would make a mistake. Multiplying is much easier—and you have been multiplying numbers for years.

Whenever you use the Slot Method, apply restrictions first. Then make the less restricted choices.

> An office manager must choose a five-digit lock code for the office door. The first and last digits of the code must be odd, and no repetition of digits is allowed. How many different lock codes are possible?

This problem is more complicated than the dinner-special problem. Some of the choices are restricted, and some choices influence the options remaining for others. In this situation, be sure to obey the following principle:

For problems in which certain choices are restricted and/or affect other choices, choose the most restricted options first.

In this problem, you *do not* want to choose the five digits in order. Instead, you should start by picking the first and last digits (which must be odd), because these digits are the most restricted. Because there are 5 different odd digits (1, 3, 5, 7, and 9), there are 5 ways of picking the first digit. Since no repetition is allowed, there are only 4 odd digits left for the last digit. You can then pick the other three digits in any order, but make sure you account for the lack of repetition. For those three choices, you have only 8, 7, and 6 digits available. Therefore, the total number of lock codes is $4 \times 5 \times 8 \times 7 \times 6 = 6,720$.

For problems like this one, in which you may end up picking "later" objects before "earlier" ones, the **Slot Method** is useful.

1) First, draw empty slots corresponding to each of the choices you have to make.

2) Then fill in each slot with the number of options for that slot. Fill in numbers *in whatever order makes the most sense*, picking the most restricted choices first.

3) Finally, following the Fundamental Counting Principle, multiply the numbers in the slots to find the total number of combinations:

For this problem, we carry out the Slot Method as follows.

First set up the slots: __ __ __ __ __

Next, fill in the restricted slots: 5   __ __ __ 4

Then fill in the remaining slots: 5   8   7   6   4

The total number of lock codes is therefore $5 \times 8 \times 7 \times 6 \times 4 = 6,720$.

*Manhattan*GMAT Prep
the new standard

Simple Factorials

You are often asked to count the possible arrangements of a set of distinct objects (e.g., "Four people sit down in 4 fixed chairs lined up in a row. How many different seating arrangements are possible?") To count these arrangements, use *factorials*:

The number of ways of putting *n* distinct objects in order, if there are no restrictions, is *n*! (*n* factorial).

The term "*n* factorial" (*n*!) refers to the product of all the positive integers from 1 through *n*, inclusive: $n! = (n)(n-1)(n-2)...(3)(2)(1)$. You should learn the factorials through 6!:

$$1! = 1 \qquad\qquad 4! = 4 \times 3 \times 2 \times 1 = 24$$
$$2! = 2 \times 1 = 2 \qquad 5! = 5 \times 4 \times 3 \times 2 \times 1 = 120$$
$$3! = 3 \times 2 \times 1 = 6 \qquad 6! = 6 \times 5 \times 4 \times 3 \times 2 \times 1 = 720$$

N! counts the rearrangements of *n* distinct objects as a special (but very common) application of the Slot Method. For example consider the case of $n = 4$, with 4 people and 4 fixed chairs. Let each slot represent a chair. Place any one of the 4 people in the first chair. You now have only 3 choices for the person in the second chair. Next, you have 2 choices for the third chair. Finally, you must put the last person in the last chair: you only have 1 choice. Now multiply together all those separate choices.

Arrangements of 4 people in 4 fixed chairs: $\underline{4} \times \underline{3} \times \underline{2} \times \underline{1} = 4! = 24$

Incidentally, you can certainly use the Slot Method the first few times to ensure that you grasp this formula, but then you should graduate to using the formula directly.

> In staging a house, a real-estate agent must place six different books on a bookshelf. In how many different orders can she arrange the books?

Using the Fundamental Counting Principle, we see that we have 6 choices for the book that goes first, 5 choices for the book that goes next, and so forth. Ultimately, we have this total:

$$6! = 6 \times 5 \times 4 \times 3 \times 2 \times 1 = 720 \text{ different orders.}$$

Anagrams

An *anagram* is a rearrangement of the letters in a word or phrase. (Puzzle enthusiasts require the rearrangement itself to be a meaningful word or phrase, but we are also going to include rearrangements that are total nonsense.) For instance, the word DEDUCTIONS is an anagram of DISCOUNTED, and so is the gibberish "word" CDDEINOSTU.

Now that you know about factorials, you can easily count the anagrams of a simple word with *n* distinct letters: simply compute *n*! (*n* factorial).

> How many different anagrams (meaningful or nonsense) are possible for the word GMAT?

Since there are 4 distinct letters in the word GMAT, there are $4! = 24$ anagrams of the word.

Although anagrams will rarely be the subject of a GMAT question, they serve as a useful model for many combinatorics problems. Consider the following problem:

> How many different anagrams (meaningful or nonsense) are possible for the word PIZZAZZ?

If you were to make an organized, exhaustive list of all the possibilities, you would find that there are 210 different anagrams—a large number, to be sure, but nowhere close to the simple factorial 7! (= 5,040), which we might expect from the 7 letters in the word PIZZAZZ.

Why are there, relatively speaking, so few anagrams? The answer lies in **repetition**: the four Z's are indistinguishable from each other. If the four Z's were all different letters, then we <u>would</u> have 7! = 5,040 different anagrams. To picture that scenario, imagine labeling the Z's with subscripts: Z_1, Z_2, Z_3, and Z_4. We could then list the 5,040 anagrams of $PIZ_1Z_2AZ_3Z_4$.

Now erase the subscripts from those 5,040 anagrams. You will notice that many "different" arrangements—like $AIPZ_1Z_2Z_3Z_4$, $AIPZ_4Z_2Z_3Z_1$, and so on—are now the <u>same</u>. In fact, for any genuinely unique anagram—like AIPZZZZ—there are now 4! = 24 identical copies in the list of 5,040 anagrams, because there are 4! = 24 ways to rearrange the four Z's in the word PIZZAZZ without changing anything. Because this 24-fold repetition occurs for *every* unique anagram of PIZZAZZ, we take 7! (which counts the arrangements *as if* the letters were all distinct) and divide by 4! (= 24) to account for the 4 repeated Z's:

$$\frac{7!}{4!} = \frac{7\times6\times5\times4\times3\times2\times1}{4\times3\times2\times1} = \frac{7\times6\times5\times\cancel{4\times3\times2\times1}}{\cancel{4\times3\times2\times1}} = 7\times6\times5 = 210$$

There are only 210 genuinely different anagrams of the word PIZZAZZ.

> How many different anagrams (meaningful or nonsense) are possible for the word ATLANTA?

As in the previous problem, the repeated letters reduce the total number of possibilities. Unlike that problem, though, this one features **multiple** repetitions: there are three A's and two T's. *Each* of these sets creates redundancy. There are 3! ways to arrange the three A's and, separately, there are 2! ways to arrange the two T's. Thus, you must divide by *each* factorial:

$$\frac{7!}{3!2!} = \frac{7\times6\times5\times4\times3\times2\times1}{(3\times2\times1)\times(2\times1)} = 7\times5\times4\times3 = 420$$

There are 420 different anagrams of the word ATLANTA.

When we have <u>repeated</u> items in the set, we <u>reduce</u> the number of arrangements.

The number of anagrams of a word is the factorial of the total number of letters, divided by the factorial(s) corresponding to each set of repeated letters.

More generally, the number of arrangements of a set of items is the factorial of the total number of items, divided by the factorial(s) corresponding to sets of indistinguishable items.

When you have repeated items, divide the "total factorial" by each "repeat factorial" to count the different arrangements.

Combinatorics with Repetition: Anagram Grids

As stated before, anagrams themselves are unlikely to appear on the GMAT. However, many combinatorics problems are exact analogues of anagram problems and can therefore be solved with the same methods developed for the two preceding problems. *Most problems involving rearranging objects can be solved by anagramming.*

> If seven people board an airport shuttle with only three available seats, how many different seating arrangements are possible? (Assume that three of the seven will actually take the seats.)

Three of the people will take the seats (designated 1, 2, and 3), and the other four will be left standing (designated "S"). The problem is therefore equivalent to finding anagrams of the "word" *123SSSS*, where the four S's are equivalent and indistinguishable. You can construct an **Anagram Grid** to help you make the connection:

Person	A	B	C	D	E	F	G
Seat	1	2	3	S	S	S	S

The top row corresponds to the 7 unique people. The bottom row corresponds to the "seating labels" that we put on those people. Note that some of these labels are repeated (the four S's). In general, you should set up an Anagram Grid to put the unique items or people on top. Only the bottom row should contain any repeated labels.

In this grid, you are free to rearrange the elements in the bottom row (the three seat numbers and the four S's), making "anagrams" that represent all the possible seating arrangements. The problem is thus identical to the PIZZAZZ problem on the last page: arranging seven elements, four of which are indistinguishable. The number of arrangements is therefore

$$\frac{7!}{4!} = \frac{7 \times 6 \times 5 \times 4 \times 3 \times 2 \times 1}{4 \times 3 \times 2 \times 1} = 7 \times 6 \times 5 = 210$$

You can also solve this problem using the Slot Method previously introduced for the lock-code problem. You do not need slots for the people left standing; you only need three slots for the actual seats.

Fill in the slots, noting that 1 person is "used up" each time: <u>7</u>   <u>6</u>   <u>5</u>

The total number of seating arrangements is therefore 7 × 6 × 5 = 210.

Now consider this problem.

> If three of seven standby passengers are selected for a flight, how many different combinations of standby passengers can be selected?

Many combinatorics problems can be solved using an anagram grid. Remember to divide by the factorial or factorials of repeated letters in the bottom row.

At first, this problem may seem identical to the previous one, because it also involves selecting 3 elements out of a set of 7. However, there is a crucial difference. This time, the three "chosen ones" are *also* indistinguishable, whereas in the earlier problem, the three seats on the shuttle were considered different. As a result, you designate all three flying passengers as *F*'s. The four non-flying passengers are still designated as *N*'s. The problem is then equivalent to finding anagrams of the "word" *FFFNNNN*. Again, you can use an Anagram Grid:

Person	A	B	C	D	E	F	G
Seat	F	F	F	N	N	N	N

To calculate the number of possibilities, we follow the same rule—factorial of the total, divided by the factorials of the repeated letters on the bottom. But notice that this grid is different from the previous one, in which we had *123NNNN* in the bottom row. Here, we divide by *two* factorials, 3! for the *F*'s and 4! for the *N*'s, yielding a much smaller number:

$$\frac{7!}{3! \times 4!} = \frac{7 \times 6 \times 5 \times 4 \times 3 \times 2 \times 1}{(3 \times 2 \times 1) \times (4 \times 3 \times 2 \times 1)} = 7 \times 5 = 35$$

The Anagram Grid works better than the Slot Method for this type of problem, which involves picking a **group** or a team with equal members. In a "pick a group" problem, we only care about who is in or out, not the internal order of the chosen group. But by their nature, slots are distinguishable. They indicate the internal order of the chosen group (one slot is first, another is second, and so on). You *can* use the Slot Method to pick groups, but you must take one extra step: divide your result by the factorial of the number in the chosen group to correct for over-counting. Or—better yet—just use the Anagram Grid!

Multiple Arrangements

So far, our discussion of combinatorics has revolved around two major topics: (1) the Fundamental Counting Principle and its implications for successive choices, and (2) the anagram approach. The GMAT will often *combine* these two ideas on more difficult combinatorics problems, requiring you to choose successive or ***multiple arrangements***.

If a GMAT problem requires you to choose two or more sets of items from separate pools, count the arrangements <u>separately</u>—perhaps using a different anagram grid each time. Then multiply the numbers of possibilities for each step.

Distinguish these problems—which require choices from *separate pools*—from complex problems that are still single arrangements (all items chosen from the *same pool*). For instance, a problem requiring the choice of a treasurer, a secretary, and three more representatives from <u>one</u> class of 20 students may seem like two or more separate problems, but it is just one: an anagram of one *T*, one *S*, three *R*'s, and fifteen *N*'s in one 20-letter "word."

> The I Eta Pi fraternity must choose a delegation of three senior members and two junior members for an annual interfraternity conference. If I Eta Pi has 12 senior members and 11 junior members, how many different delegations are possible?

To count possible groups, divide the total factorial by **two** factorials: one for the chosen group and one for those not chosen.

This problem involves two genuinely different arrangements: three seniors chosen from a pool of 12 seniors, and two juniors chosen from a *separate* pool of 11 juniors. These arrangements should be calculated separately.

Because the three spots in the delegation are not distinguishable, choosing the seniors is equivalent to choosing an anagram of three Y's and nine N's, which can be accomplished in $\dfrac{12!}{9! \times 3!} = 220$ different ways. Similarly, choosing the juniors is equivalent to choosing an anagram of two Y's and nine N's, which can be done in $\dfrac{11!}{9! \times 2!} = 55$ different ways.

Since the choices are successive and independent, multiply the numbers: $220 \times 55 = 12{,}100$ different delegations are possible.

Arrangements with Constraints

The most complex combinatorics problems include unusual constraints: one person refuses to sit next to another, for example.

> Greg, Marcia, Peter, Jan, Bobby, and Cindy go to a movie and sit next to each other in 6 adjacent seats in the front row of the theater. If Marcia and Jan will not sit next to each other, in how many different arrangements can the six people sit?

This is a simple arrangement with one unusual constraint: Marcia and Jan will not sit next to each other. To solve the problem, ignore the constraint for now. Just find the number of ways in which six people can sit in 6 chairs.

$$6! = 6 \times 5 \times 4 \times 3 \times 2 \times 1 = 720$$

Because of the constraint on Jan and Marcia, though, not all of those 720 seating arrangements are viable. So you should count the arrangements in which Jan *is* sitting next to Marcia (the *undesirable* seating arrangements), and subtract them from the total of 720.

To count the ways in which Jan *must* sit next to Marcia, use the **Glue Method**:

For problems in which items or people must be next to each other, pretend that the items "stuck together" are actually one larger item.

We imagine that Jan and Marcia are "stuck together" into one person. There are now effectively 5 "people": JM (stuck together), G, P, B, and C. The arrangements can now be counted. These 5 "people" can be arranged in $5! = 120$ different ways.

Each of those 120 different ways, though, represents *two* different possibilities, because the "stuck together" moviegoers could be in order either as J–M or as M–J. Therefore, the total number of seating arrangements with Jan next to Marcia is $2 \times 120 = 240$.

Finally, do not forget that those 240 possibilities are the ones to be *excluded* from consideration. The number of allowed seating arrangements is therefore $720 - 240$, or 480.

If the problem has unusual constraints, try counting arrangements without constraints first. Then subtract the forbidden arrangements.

Combination and Permutation Formulas (Advanced)

Many of the situations put forward in previous problems fall under the general umbrella of *combinations* and *permutations*. If you can distinguish clearly between the two concepts and apply them efficiently to problems, you can save a great deal of time. Note that you can solve the vast majority of GMAT combinatorics problems using the methods described above. The formulas below may be primarily considered time-savers.

A **combination** is a selection of items from a larger pool. In a combination, **the order of items does not matter**. In other words, the three-item combinations of items A–B–C and B–C–A are considered identical. Think teams or groups: all that matters is who is in and who is out. The winners are considered indistinguishable.

If the order does not matter, use the letters Y and N to represent Yes and No situations.

A **permutation** is also a selection of items from a larger pool. In a permutation, however, **the order of items matters**. In other words, the permutations A–B–C and B–A–C are considered distinct. Think seating arrangements or Olympic medal ceremonies: what matters is not only who gets a seat or a medal, but also <u>which</u> seat or medal each winner gets. The winners are considered distinguishable.

Here are the formulas:

The number of **combinations** of r items, chosen from a pool of n items, is

$$\frac{n!}{(n-r)! \cdot r!}$$

The number of **permutations** of r items, chosen from a pool of n items, is

$$\frac{n!}{(n-r)!}$$

As a special case, the number of permutations of all n items in a pool of n items is just $n!$, just as we saw at the beginning of the chapter. (You can use the general permutation formula for this special case, as long as you remember that $0! = 1$.)

These formulas are considerably more "user-friendly" than they might at first appear, because their entire denominators will always cancel, leaving behind an integer. (You cannot have fractional numbers of possibilities!) You must be *extremely* careful that you are using the correct formula, though. Many GMAT *combination* problems feature incorrect answers corresponding to the use of *permutations*, and vice versa. **If switching the elements in a chosen set creates a different set, it is a permutation. If not, it is a combination.**

Note that there are usually fewer combinations than permutations. As we saw before, there are 210 permutations of 3 items chosen from a pool of 7 distinct items, but there are only 35 combinations of 3 items chosen from the same pool. The combination formula is the permutation formula divided by one more term: $r!$, the factorial of the number of chosen items. If you only choose 1 item, then the number of combinations is the same as the number of permutations, since $1! = 1$. But if you choose more than 1 item, the number of combinations will be less than the number of permutations.

Be aware of the difference between combinations ("order does not matter") and permutations ("order matters") in considering the following problem.

> Three small cruise ships, each carrying 10 passengers, will dock tomorrow. One ship will dock at Port A, another at Port B, and the third at Port C. At Port A, two passengers will be selected at random; each winner will receive one gift certificate worth $50. At Port B, one passenger will be selected at random to receive a gift certificate worth $35, and at Port C, one passenger will be selected at random to receive a gift certificate worth $25. How many different ways can the gift certificates be given out?

This problem features four separate decisions. In other words, you must answer four separate questions:

Use this method to solve more complex combination and permutation problems.

(1)   Which ship docks at which port?
(2)   Who are the two people who receive the two gift certificates at Port A?
(3)   Who receives the one gift certificate at Port B?
(4)   Who receives the one gift certificate at Port C?

The first of these decisions is a *permutation*, because "order matters." In other words, switching any of the port assignments results in a new arrangement.

This arrangement is different from	*Ship 1 at Port A*	*Ship 2 at Port B*	*Ship 3 at Port C*
this arrangement	*Ship 1 at Port B*	*Ship 2 at Port A*	*Ship 3 at Port C*

Since the gift certificates are worth different amounts at different ports, the specific way in which we assign ships to ports matters.

Thus, we calculate the number of permutations of the 3 ships over the 3 ports as $3! = 6$.

The second decision is a *combination*, because "order does not matter." You do not care about the sequence in which you choose the two winners. You only care about who has won. Since there are 2 winners and $10 - 2 = 8$ losers out of a pool of 10 contestants at Port A, we can write the number of combinations as $\dfrac{10!}{2! \times (10-2)!} = \dfrac{10 \times 9}{2} = 45$.

Finally, the third and fourth decisions are very simple combinations. You have 10 choices for who receives the certificate at Port B, and separately you have 10 choices for who receives the certificate at Port C.

The decisions are sequential, and they are made independently. As a result, the numbers of possibilities are multiplied at the end of the problem. The total number of ways the gift certificates can be given out is therefore

$$(3!) \times \left(\frac{10!}{2! \times (10-2)!} \right) \times 10 \times 10 = 6 \times 45 \times 10 \times 10 = 27,000$$

Disguised Combinatorics (Advanced)

Most GMAT combinatorics problems lack pretense. For instance, the problem might literally focus on selecting a group of 3 students from a pool of 10 students. However, you will see some combinatorics problems in disguise, with problem statements that seem to bear little resemblance to the typical examples shown so far in this chapter.

Many word problems involving the words "how many" are combinatorics problems. Also, many combinatorics problems masquerade as probability problems. The difficult part of the problem draws on combinatorics to count desired or total possibilities, whereas creating the probability fraction is trivial. If you think creatively enough, looking for *analogies* to known problem types, you will probably be able to find a viable combinatorics solution.

Here are some examples of combinatorics problems that at first may appear to have little to do with combinatorics:

- How many four-digit integers have digits with some specified properties?
- How many paths exist from point A to point B in a given diagram?
- How many diagonals, triangles, lines, etc. exist in a given geometrical figure?
- How many *pairings* (handshakes, games between two teams, nonstop flights between cities, etc.) exist in a given situation? (Pairings are groups of 2.)

As noted above, any of these problems may be *further* disguised in the cloak of probability—which may even hide *two* combinatorics problems (one for the numerator of the probability fraction and one for the denominator) in one question!

Here is an example:

> Alicia lives in a town whose streets are on a grid system, with all streets running east–west or north–south without breaks. Her school, located on a corner, lies three blocks south and three blocks east of his home, also located on a corner. If Alicia is equally likely to choose any possible path from home to school, and if she only walks south or east, what is the probability that she will walk south for the first two blocks?

Draw a diagram of the situation:

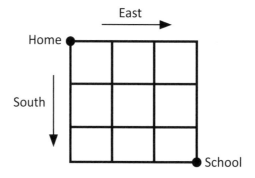

Do not worry if you do not recognize the problem right away. Simply read and understand the problem first.

If you are an extremely organized artist, you may choose to sketch out all the different paths. But that approach has several drawbacks:

1) It is time-consuming. You do not know the number of paths at the outset—for all you know, there could be hundreds.

2) It is fraught with danger. Missing even one possible path is fatal.

3) It is cumbersome—especially on the ungainly yellow pad you will be given at the testing site.

Instead, you should recognize this problem for what it is: a simple combinatorics problem in a cheap tuxedo. Think back to the Fundamental Counting Principle, in which you analyze a big, complex decision as the product of several separate decisions. For instance, the choice of sandwich was analyzed as the product of two simpler decisions: choice of bread and choice of filling. So you need to figure out what the simple, step-wise decisions are.

To start walking, Alicia must choose either to walk South or to walk East. After one block, she is faced with the same decision: to walk South or to walk East. Now, as she continues, she runs into constraints. For instance, she may no longer be able to walk South at a certain point. But we should still regard the basic, step-wise decision as South or East.

How many of these decisions does she have to make (even if some are cut off later on)? The answer is 6: she has to walk 6 blocks overall.

Finally, we think about the constraints. To get home, Alicia must walk exactly three blocks South and three blocks East; the only issue is the order in which she does so. If *S* represents South and *E* represents East, then *SSSEEE* represents one possible path. *ESESSE* represents another path.

Therefore, the problem involves anagramming three *S*'s and three *E*'s. Remember:

$$\text{Probability} = \frac{\text{\# of desired possibilities}}{\text{Total \# of possibilities}}$$

The denominator of this fraction is the number of anagrams of three *E*'s and three *S*'s, which is $\dfrac{6!}{3! \times 3!} = 20$. Alicia can take any of 20 different paths from home to school. Notice how much easier this computation is than drawing out all 20 possible paths!

The numerator of the probability fraction is the number of anagrams of three *E*'s and three *S*'s *with two S's always coming first*. Since you cannot change the first two letters, **just ignore them**. This technique of **Reducing the Pool** is akin to the Glue Method. Here, we are *reducing the pool* from 6 letters to 4, by gluing the first two *S*'s to their spots permanently. The probability numerator is therefore the number of anagrams of three *E*'s and one *S*, which is $\dfrac{4!}{3! \times 1!} = 4$. Only four of Alicia's possible paths to school satisfy the problem's requirement. The desired probability is therefore 4/20 = 1/5.

Notice that the answer is NOT 1/4, as if Alicia flipped a coin at each of the two junctures to decide which way to go! Rather, she is choosing from among all possible paths equally.

Break down complicated counting problems into separate decisions made step by step. Then use this chapter's techniques.

Problem Set

Solve the following problems, using the strategies you have learned in this section.

1. In how many different ways can the letters in the word "LEVEL" be arranged?

2. Amy and Adam are making boxes of truffles to give out as wedding favors. They have an unlimited supply of 5 different types of truffles. If each box holds 2 truffles of different types, how many different boxes can they make?

3. A men's basketball league assigns every player a two-digit number for the back of his jersey. If the league uses only the digits 1–5, what is the maximum number of players that can join the league such that no player has a number with a repeated digit (e.g. 22), and no two players have the same number?

4. The security gate at a storage facility requires a five-digit lock code. If the lock code must consist only of digits from 1 through 7, inclusive, with no repeated digits, and the first and last digits of the code must be odd, how many lock codes are possible?

5. The Natural Woman, a women's health food store, offers its own blends of trail mix. If the store uses 4 different ingredients, how many bins will it need to hold every possible blend, assuming that each blend must have at least two ingredients? (Also assume that each bin can hold one and only one blend.)

6. A pod of 6 dolphins always swims single file, with 3 females at the front and 3 males in the rear. In how many different arrangements can the dolphins swim?

7. A delegation from Gotham City goes to Metropolis to discuss a limited Batman–Superman partnership. If the mayor of Metropolis chooses 3 members of the 7-person delegation to meet with Superman, how many different 3-person combinations can he choose?

8. A British spy is trying to escape from his prison cell. The lock requires him to enter one number, from 1–9, and then push a pair of colored buttons simultaneously. He can make one attempt every 3 seconds. If there are 6 colored buttons, what is the longest possible time it could take the spy to escape from the prison cell?

9. The New York Classical Group is designing the liner notes for an upcoming CD release. There are 10 soloists featured on the album, but the liner notes are only 5 pages long, and therefore only have room for 5 of the soloists. The soloists are fighting over which of them will appear in the liner notes, as well as who will be featured on which page. How many different liner note arrangements are possible?

10. The principal of a high school needs to schedule observations of 6 teachers. She plans to visit one teacher each day for a workweek (Monday through Friday), so she will only have time to see 5 of the teachers. How many different observation schedules can she create?

11. A second grade class is writing reports on birds. The students' teacher has given them a list of 6 birds they can choose to write about. If Lizzie wants to write a report that includes two or three of the birds, how many different reports can she write?

12. Every morning, Casey walks from her house to the bus stop, as shown to the right. She always travels exactly nine blocks from her house to the bus, but she varies the route she takes every day. (One sample route is shown.) How many days can Casey walk from her house to the bus stop without repeating the same route?

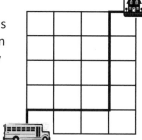

13. A mother bird has 6 babies. Every time she returns to the nest, she feeds half the babies, even if some of those babies were fed the last time around. If it takes her 5 minutes to feed each baby, how long will it take her to feed all the possible combinations of three babies? Leave out the time the mother bird spends away from the nest.

14. Mario's Pizza has two choices of crust: deep dish and thin-and-crispy. The restaurant also has a choice of 5 toppings: tomatoes, sausage, peppers, onions, and pepperoni. Finally, Mario's offers every pizza in extra-cheese as well as regular. If Linda's volleyball team decides to order a pizza with four toppings, how many different choices do the teammates have at Mario's Pizza?

15. Three gnomes and three elves sit down in a row of six chairs. If no gnome will sit next to another gnome and no elf will sit next to another elf, in how many different ways can the elves and gnomes sit?

16. Gordon buys 5 dolls for his 5 nieces. The gifts include two identical Sun-and-Fun beach dolls, one Elegant Eddie dress-up doll, one G.I. Josie army doll, and one Tulip Troll doll. If the youngest niece does not want the G.I. Josie doll, in how many different ways can he give the gifts?

17. The students at Natural High School sell coupon books to raise money for after-school programs. At the end of the coupon sale, the school selects six students to win prizes as follows: From the homeroom with the highest total coupon-book sales, the students with the first-, second- and third-highest sales receive $50, $30, and $20, respectively; from the homeroom with the second-highest total coupon-book sales, the three highest-selling students receive $10 each. If Natural High School has ten different homerooms with eight students each, in how many different ways could the six prizes be awarded? (Assume that there are no ties, either among students or among homerooms.) Write your answer as a product of primes raised to various powers (do not actually compute the number).

1. **30:** There are two repeated E's and two repeated L's in the word "LEVEL." To find the anagrams for this word, set up a fraction in which the numerator is the factorial of the number of letters and the denominator is the factorial of the number of each repeated letter.

$$\frac{5!}{2!2!} = \frac{5 \times 4 \times 3 \times 2 \times 1}{2 \times 1 \times 2 \times 1} = 30$$

Alternatively, you can solve this problem using the Slot Method, as long as you correct for over-counting (since you have some indistinguishable elements). There are five choices for the first letter, four for the second, and so on, making the product $5 \times 4 \times 3 \times 2 \times 1 = 120$. However, there are two sets of 2 indistinguishable elements each, so you must divide by 2! to account for each of these. Thus, the total number of combinations is $\dfrac{5 \times 4 \times 3 \times 2 \times 1}{2! \times 2!} = 30$.

2. **10:** In every combination, two types of truffles will be in the box, and three types of truffles will not. Therefore, this problem is a question about the number of anagrams that can be made from the "word" YYNNN:

$$\frac{5!}{2!3!} = \frac{5 \times 4 \times 3 \times 2 \times 1}{3 \times 2 \times 1 \times 2 \times 1} = 5 \times 2 = 10$$

A	B	C	D	E
Y	Y	N	N	N

This problem can also be solved with the formula for combinations, since it is a combination of two items chosen from a set of five (in which order does not matter). Therefore, there are $\dfrac{5!}{2! \times 3!} = 10$ possible combinations.

3. **20:** In this problem, the order of the numbers matters. Each number can be either the tens digit, the units digit, or not a digit in the number. Therefore, this problem is a question about the number of anagrams that can be made from the "word" TUNNN:

$$\frac{5!}{3!} = \frac{5 \times 4 \times 3 \times 2 \times 1}{3 \times 2 \times 1} = 5 \times 4 = 20$$

1	2	3	4	5
T	U	N	N	N

This problem can also be solved with the formula for permutations. The situation is a permutation of two items chosen from a set of five (order matters this time, since switching the two digits produces a genuinely different jersey number).

Therefore, there are $\dfrac{5!}{(5-2)!} = \dfrac{5!}{3!} = 20$ possible permutations. (Remember, in the permutation formula, you always divide, not by the factorial of the number chosen, but by the factorial of the number NOT chosen.)

You can also use the slot method. The slots correspond to the positions of the digits (tens and units). You have 5 choices for the tens digit and then only 4 choices for the units digit (since you cannot use the same digit again), resulting in $5 \times 4 = 20$ possibilities. This method works well for problems in which order matters.

Finally, you can just list out the jersey numbers, since the number of possibilities is low. Even if you stop partway through, this can be a good way to start, so that you get a sense of the problem.

12, 13, 14, 15, 21, 23, 24, 25, 31, 32, 34, 35, 41, 42, 43, 45, 51, 52, 53, 54 = 5 groups of 4 = 20.

*Manhattan*GMAT*Prep

4. 720: This problem is a permutation, since "order matters"; that is, all the digits in the code are distinguishable from each other. Furthermore, because of the restrictions on the first and last digits, it cannot be solved with the anagram method (which only works for unrestricted choices of sub-sets from some larger pool). Therefore, the Slot Method is the best method of solution. Begin with the most restricted choices: the first and last digits. There are 4 choices for the first digit, because there are 4 odd digits available (1, 3, 5, 7); there are 3 choices for the last digit, because whatever digit was chosen first cannot be repeated.

$$\underline{\quad 4 \quad} \qquad \underline{\qquad} \qquad \underline{\qquad} \qquad \underline{\qquad} \qquad \underline{\quad 3 \quad}$$

After these two decisions, the rest of the choices are unrestricted, so there are 5, 4, and 3 choices, respectively, remaining for the second, third, and fourth digits of the lock code:

$$\underline{\quad 4 \quad} \qquad \underline{\quad 5 \quad} \qquad \underline{\quad 4 \quad} \qquad \underline{\quad 3 \quad} \qquad \underline{\quad 3 \quad}$$

The total number of lock codes is therefore $4 \times 5 \times 4 \times 3 \times 3 = 720$.

5. 11: Trail mix blends can contain either 2, 3, or 4 ingredients. Consider each case separately. First, figure out the number of 2-ingredient blends as anagrams of the "word" YYNN:

A	B	C	D
Y	Y	N	N

$$\frac{4!}{2!2!} = \frac{4 \times 3 \times 2 \times 1}{2 \times 1 \times 2 \times 1} = 2 \times 3 = 6$$

Then, consider the number of 3-ingredient blends as anagrams of the "word" YYYN:

A	B	C	D
Y	Y	Y	N

$$\frac{4!}{3!} = \frac{4 \times 3 \times 2 \times 1}{3 \times 2 \times 1} = 4$$

Finally, consider the unique blend that includes all 4 ingredients. All in all, there are $6 + 4 + 1 = 11$ blends. The store will need 11 bins to hold all the blends.

You can also solve this problem by using the formula for combinations 3 separate times: once for all combinations of 2 different flavors, once for all combinations of 3 different flavors, and once for all combinations of 4 different flavors. Note that all of these are combinations, not permutations, because the order of the different flavors is immaterial.

Therefore, the number of bins required is $\dfrac{4!}{2! \times 2!} + \dfrac{4!}{3! \times 1!} + \dfrac{4!}{4! \times 0!} = 6 + 4 + 1 = 11$. (Recall that $0! = 1$.)

6. 36: There are 3! ways in which the 3 females can swim. There are 3! ways in which the 3 males can swim. Therefore, there are $3! \times 3!$ ways in which the entire pod can swim:

$$3! \times 3! = 6 \times 6 = 36.$$

This is a multiple arrangements problem, in which we have 2 separate pools (females and males).

7. **35:** Model this problem with anagrams for the "word" YYYNNNN, in which three people are in the delegation and 4 are not:

$$\frac{7!}{3!4!} = \frac{7 \times 6 \times 5}{3 \times 2 \times 1} = 35$$ Note that you must divide by both 3! and 4! in this problem.

Alternatively, you can use the combination formula, because this problem requires the number of possible combinations of 3 delegates taken from a total of 7.

A	B	C	D	E	F	G
Y	Y	Y	N	N	N	N

(Note that order does not matter.) Therefore, the number of possible combinations is $\frac{7!}{3! \times 4!} = 35$.

8. **6.75 minutes:** First, consider how many different pairs of colored buttons there are with the anagram YYNNNN:

$$\frac{6!}{4!2!} = \frac{6 \times 5 \times 4 \times 3 \times 2 \times 1}{4 \times 3 \times 2 \times 1 \times 2 \times 1} = 3 \times 5 = 15$$

A	B	C	D	E	F
Y	Y	N	N	N	N

For each number the spy tries, he must then try all 15 button combinations. Therefore, there are 15 tries per number. With 9 numbers, there are $15 \times 9 = 135$ tries. If each try takes 3 seconds, it will take the spy a maximum of $135 \times 3 = 405$ seconds, or 6.75 minutes, to escape from the cell.

You can also find the number of different combinations of colored buttons with the combinations formula, because order does not matter (the buttons are pressed simultaneously): $\frac{6!}{2! \times 4!} = 15$ combinations.

9. **30,240:** In this problem, the order in which the soloists appear is important. Therefore, the problem can be modeled with anagrams of the "word" 12345NNNNN, in which each number represents the page on which a soloist might appear:

A	B	C	D	E	F	G	H	I	J
1	2	3	4	5	N	N	N	N	N

$$\frac{10!}{5!} = 10 \times 9 \times 8 \times 7 \times 6 = 30,240$$

This expression $\frac{10!}{5!}$ is also the result of using the permutation formula $\frac{10!}{(10-5)!}$, since five soloists are chosen from an overall set of ten (and *order matters*, because they are assigned to different numbered pages). Remember that the 5! in the denominator corresponds to the 5 soloists NOT chosen.

Alternatively, you can use the slot method. The slots correspond to the pages in the liner notes. You have 10 choices for the soloist on the first page, 9 choices for the soloist on the second page, 8 choices for the soloist on the third page, and so on. Multiplying the separate numbers of choices together, you get $10 \times 9 \times 8 \times 7 \times 6 = 30,240$ total possibilities.

10. **720:** Model this problem with anagrams of the "word" 12345N, in which each teacher could be visited first, second, third, fourth, fifth, or not at all.

A	B	C	D	E	F
1	2	3	4	5	N

$6! = 6 \times 5 \times 4 \times 3 \times 2 \times 1 = 720$ Do not divide, since no letters are repeated.

You can also use the permutation formula again: the principal is choosing a set of five teachers from a total of six, and *order matters* (because they are placed on different days in the schedule). Therefore, the total number of observation schedules is $\dfrac{6!}{(6-5)!} = \dfrac{6!}{1!} = 720$.

Notice that the answer is equal to 6! = 720. You have the same number of possibilities when you schedule 5 out of 6 teachers (and leave one out) as when you schedule all 6 teachers. The "left-out" teacher in the first situation can simply be thought of as being scheduled on a different day from all the others in the second situation. This equivalence occurs when order matters AND you have just ONE "odd man out" (in other words, you are arranging $n - 1$ distinct people out of n people).

11. **35:** First, figure out the number of 2-bird reports as anagrams of the "word" YYNNNN:

$\dfrac{6!}{4!2!} = \dfrac{6 \times 5}{2 \times 1} = 15$

A	B	C	D	E	F
Y	Y	N	N	N	N

Then, consider the number of 3-bird reports as anagrams of the "word" YYYNNN:

$\dfrac{6!}{3!3!} = \dfrac{6 \times 5 \times 4}{3 \times 2 \times 1} = 20$

A	B	C	D	E	F
Y	Y	Y	N	N	N

All in all, there are 15 + 20 = 35 possible bird combinations.

These expressions may also be found from two direct applications of the combinations formula (because the order in which the birds are presented in the report is immaterial):

$\dfrac{6!}{3! \times 3!} + \dfrac{6!}{2! \times 4!} = 20 + 15 = 35$

12. **126:** No matter which route Casey walks, she will travel 4 blocks to the left and 5 blocks down. This can be modeled with the "word" LLLLDDDDD. Find the number of anagrams for this "word":

$\dfrac{9!}{5!4!} = \dfrac{9 \times 8 \times 7 \times 6}{4 \times 3 \times 2 \times 1} = 126$

This problem can also be solved with the *combinations* formula. Casey is going to walk 9 blocks in a row, no matter what. Imagine that those blocks are already marked 1, 2, 3, 4, (the first block she walks, the second block she walks, and so on), up to 9. Now, to create a route, four of those blocks will be dubbed "Left" and the other five will be "Down." The question is, in how many ways can she assign those labels to the numbered blocks?

The answer is given by the fact that she is choosing a combination of either 4 blocks out of 9 ("Left") or 5 blocks out of 9 ("Down"). (Either method gives the same answer.) At first it may seem as though "order matters" here, because Casey is choosing routes, but "order" does not matter in the combinatorial sense. That is, designating blocks 1, 2, 3, and 4 as "Left" blocks is the same as designating blocks 3, 2, 4, and 1 as "Left" blocks (or any other order of those same four blocks). Therefore, use combinations, not permutations, to derive the expressions: $\dfrac{9!}{5! \times 4!} = 126$.

13. **5 hours:** The mother bird can feed 3 babies out of six. Model this situation with the "word" YYYNNN. Find the number of anagrams for this word:

$$\frac{6!}{3!3!} = \frac{6 \times 5 \times 4}{3 \times 2 \times 1} = 20$$

1	2	3	4	5	6
Y	Y	Y	N	N	N

If it takes 5 minutes to feed each baby, it will take 15 minutes to feed each combination of babies. Thus, it will take $20 \times 15 = 300$ minutes, or 5 hours, to feed all the possible combinations.

Alternatively, use the combinations formula to find the number of different combinations of three birds out of six (because the order of the birds does not matter): $\dfrac{6!}{3! \times 3!} = 20$.

14. **20:** Consider the toppings first. Model the toppings with the "word" YYYYN, in which four of the toppings are on the pizza and one is not. The number of anagrams for this "word" is:

$$\frac{5!}{4!} = 5$$

A	B	C	D	E
Y	Y	Y	Y	N

If each of these pizzas can also be offered in 2 choices of crust, there are $5 \times 2 = 10$ pizzas. The same logic applies for extra-cheese and regular: $10 \times 2 = 20$.

Alternatively, use the combinations formula to count the combinations of toppings: $\dfrac{5!}{4! \times 1!} = 5$. Or use an intuitive approach: choosing four toppings out of five is equivalent to choosing the ONE topping that will not be on the pizza. There are clearly 5 ways to do that.

15. **72:** The only way to ensure that no two gnomes and no two elves sit next to each other is to have the gnomes and elves alternate seats (GEGEGE or EGEGEG). Use the Slot Method to assign seats to gnomes or elves. Begin by seating the first gnome. As he is the first to be seated, he can sit anywhere. He has 6 choices. If the first gnome sits in an odd-numbered chair, the second

Person	Choices	Seat Assigned
Gnome A	6 choices (1, 2, 3, 4, 5, 6)	#1
Gnome B	2 choices (3, 5)	#3
Gnome C	1 choice (5)	#5
Elf A	3 choices (2, 4, 6)	#2
Elf B	2 choices (4, 6)	#4
Elf C	1 choice (6)	#6

gnome can sit in either of the two remaining odd-numbered chairs. (Likewise, if the first gnome sits in an even-numbered chair, the second gnome can sit in either of the two remaining even-numbered chairs.)

Either way, the second gnome has two choices. The last gnome has only 1 chair option, since she is not to be seated next to another gnome.

Then, seat the elves. The first elf can sit in any of the three empty chairs, the second in any of the other two, and the last in the final remaining chair. Therefore, the first elf has three choices, the second elf has two choices, and the third elf has one choice.

Finally, find the product of the number of choices for each "person":

$$6 \times 2 \times 1 \times 3 \times 2 \times 1 = 72$$

You can also think of this problem as a succession of three choices: (1) choosing whether to arrange the little guys as DEDEDE or EDEDED, (2) choosing the order of the gnomes, and then (3) choosing the order of the elves.

The first choice has only two options: EDEDED and DEDEDE. Each of the subsequent choices has 3! = 6 options, because those choices involve unrestricted rearrangements (Simple Factorials). Therefore, the total number of seating arrangements is $2 \times 3! \times 3! = 2 \times 6 \times 6 = 72$.

16. **48:** First, solve the problem without considering the fact that the youngest girl does not want the G.I. Josie doll.

Gordon's nieces could get either one of the Sun-and-Fun dolls, which we will call S. Or they could get the Elegant Eddie doll (E), the Tulip Troll doll (T), or the G.I. Josie doll (G). This problem can be modeled with anagrams for the "word" SSETG.

$$\frac{5!}{2!} = 5 \times 4 \times 3 = 60$$

A	B	C	D	E
S	S	E	T	G

Divide by 2! because of the two identical Sun-and-Fun dolls.

There are 60 ways in which Gordon can give the gifts to his nieces.

However, we know that the youngest girl (niece E) does not want the G.I. Josie doll. So, we calculate the number of arrangements in which the youngest girl DOES get the G.I. Josie doll. If niece E gets doll G, then we still have 2 S dolls, 1 E doll, and 1 T doll to give out to nieces A, B, C, and D. Model this situation with the anagrams of the "word" SSET:

$$\frac{4!}{2!} = 12$$

A	B	C	D
S	S	E	T

There are 12 ways in which the youngest niece WILL get the G.I. Josie doll.

Therefore, there are 60 − 12 = 48 ways in which Gordon can give the dolls to his nieces.

17. $(2^8)(3^3)(5)(7^2)$: There are three separate sets of decisions to be made in this problem. You can think of these decisions as questions to answer. First, which two homerooms have the highest total sales? Second, who are the three highest-selling students from the first-place homeroom? Third, who are the three highest-selling students from the second-place homeroom? In each of these decisions, the crucial issue is whether order matters. In other words, does switching the order of the choices have any effect on the result? If switching the order matters, the choice is that of a "permutation." If switching does not matter, the choice is that of a "combination."

First, choose the two homerooms. Here, order matters, because the first-place homeroom receives different prizes than does the second-place homeroom. The slot method (fundamental counting principle) is simplest: the two homerooms can be chosen in 10×9 different ways. (Do not bother computing the product, even though it is easy to do, because we are going to factor down to primes anyway.) The anagram method works too, using

anagrams of the "word" 12NNNNNNNN: $\dfrac{10!}{(8!)(1!)(1!)} = 10 \times 9$.

Second, select the three prize winners from the first-place homeroom. Here, order also matters, because the three selected students receive three different prizes. The slot method (fundamental counting principle) is simplest again: $8 \times 7 \times 6$ different ways. Alternatively, use the anagram method with the "word" 123NNNNN:

$\dfrac{8!}{(5!)(1!)(1!)(1!)} = 8 \times 7 \times 6$.

Finally, select the three prize winners from the second-place homeroom. In this case, order does not matter, because the same prize is given to each of the three winning students. Therefore, this is a combination, using the

anagram method for the "word" YYYNNNNN: $\dfrac{8!}{(5!)(3!)} = 8 \times 7$ different ways.

Since these three decisions are sequential, the total number of ways in which the winners can be chosen is:

$$(10 \times 9)(8 \times 7 \times 6)(8 \times 7) = (2 \times 5 \times 3^2)(2^3 \times 7 \times 2 \times 3)(2^3 \times 7)$$
$$= 2^8 \times 3^3 \times 5 \times 7^2$$

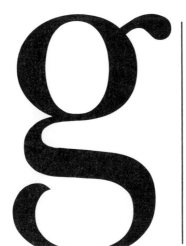

Chapter 5
of
WORD TRANSLATIONS

PROBABILITY

In This Chapter . . .

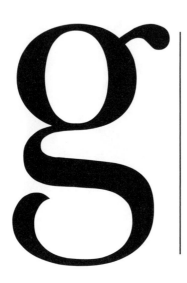

- "1" Is the Greatest Probability

- More than One Event: "AND" vs. "OR"

- The $1 - x$ Probability Trick

- The Domino Effect

- Probability Trees

- Combinatorics and Probability (Advanced)

- Combinatorics and The Domino Effect (Advanced)

- Reformulating Difficult Problems (Advanced)

PROBABILITY

Probability is a quantity that expresses the chance, or likelihood, of an event. In other words, it measures how often an event will occur in a long series of repeated trials.

For events with countable outcomes, probability is defined as the following fraction:

$$\text{Probability} = \frac{\text{Number of } \textit{desired} \text{ or } \textit{successful} \text{ outcomes}}{\text{Total number of } \textit{possible} \text{ outcomes}}$$

As a simple illustration, rolling a die has **six** possible outcomes: 1, 2, 3, 4, 5, and 6. The probability of rolling a "5" is 1/6, because the "5" corresponds to only **one** of those outcomes. The probability of rolling a prime number, though, is 3/6 = 1/2, because in that case, three of the outcomes (2, 3, and 5) are considered successes.

For the probability fraction to be meaningful, all the outcomes must be **equally likely**. One might say, for instance, that the lottery has only two outcomes"—win or lose—but that does not mean the probability of winning the lottery is 1/2. If you want to calculate the correct probability of winning the lottery, you must find out how many *equally likely outcomes* are possible. In other words, you have to count up all the specific combinations of different numbered balls.

> To find a probability, you need to know the total number of possibilities and the number of **successful scenarios**.

In some problems, you will have to think carefully about how to break a situation down into equally likely outcomes. Consider the following problem:

> If a fair coin is tossed three times, what is the probability that it will turn up heads exactly twice?

You may be tempted to say that there are four possibilities—no heads, 1 head, 2 heads, and 3 heads—and that the probability of 2 heads is thus ¼. You would be wrong, though, because those four outcomes are not equally likely. You are much more likely to get 1 or 2 heads than to get all heads or all tails. Instead, you have to formulate equally likely outcomes in terms of the outcome of each flip:

HHH   HHT   HTH   THH   HTT   THT   TTH   TTT

If you have trouble formulating this list from scratch, you can use a **counting tree**, which breaks down possible outcomes step by step, with only one decision at each branch of the tree.

These eight outcomes are equally likely, because the coin is equally likely to come up heads or tails at each flip. Three outcomes on this list (HHT, HTH, THH) have heads exactly twice, so the probability of exactly two heads is 3/8.

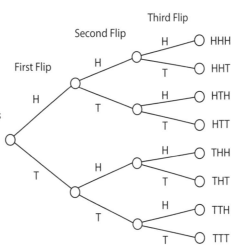

This result can be written thus:

P(exactly 2 heads) = 3/8

"1" is the Greatest Probability

The greatest probability—the certainty that an event will occur—is 1. Thus, a probability of 1 means that the event must occur. For example:

The probability that you roll a fair die once, and it lands on a number less than seven, is certain, or 1.

$$\frac{\text{Number of } \textit{successful} \text{ outcomes}}{\text{Total number of possible outcomes}} = \frac{6}{6} = \mathbf{1}$$

As a percent, this certainty is expressed as 100%.

The converse is also true. The lowest probability—the impossibility that an event will occur—is 0. Thus, a probability of 0 means that an event will NOT occur. For example, the probability that you roll a fair die once and it lands on the number 9 is impossible, or 0.

$$\frac{\text{Number of } \textit{successful} \text{ outcomes}}{\text{Total number of possible outcomes}} = \frac{0}{6} = \mathbf{0}$$

As a percent, this impossibility is expressed as 0%. Thus, probabilities can be percents between 0% and 100%, inclusive, or fractions between 0 and 1, inclusive.

More than One Event: "AND" vs. "OR"

Probability problems that deal with multiple events usually involve two operations: multiplication and addition. The key to understanding probability is to understand when you must multiply and when you must add.

1) Assume that X and Y are independent events. **To determine the probability that event X AND event Y will both occur, MULTIPLY the two probabilities together.**

> What is the probability that a fair coin flipped twice will land on heads both times?

This is an "AND" problem, because it is asking for the probability that the coin will land on heads on the first flip AND on the second flip. The probability that the coin will land on heads on the first flip is 1/2. The probability that the coin will land on heads on the second flip is 1/2.

Therefore, the probability that the coin will land on heads on both flips is $\frac{1}{2} \times \frac{1}{2} = \frac{1}{4}$.

Note that the probability of having BOTH flips come up heads (1/4) is less than the probability of just one flip come up heads (1/2). This should make intuitive sense. If you define success in a more constrained way (e.g., "to win, BOTH this AND that have to happen"), then the probability of success will be lower. The operation of multiplication should also make sense. Typical probabilities are fractions between 0 and 1. When you multiply together two such fractions, you make a *smaller* product.

AND means multiply the probabilities. You will wind up with a smaller number, which indicates a lower probability of success.

*Manhattan*GMAT*Prep
the new standard

2) Assume that *X* and *Y* are independent events and that they are mutually exclusive events (meaning that the two events cannot both occur). **To determine the probability that event *X* OR event *Y* will occur, ADD the two probabilities together.**

> What is the probability that a fair die rolled once will land on either 4 or 5?

This is an "OR" problem, because it is asking for the probability that the die will land on either 4 **or** 5. The probability that the die will land on 4 is 1/6. The probability that the die will land on 5 is 1/6.

Therefore, the probability that the die will land on either 4 or 5 is $\frac{1}{6} + \frac{1}{6} = \frac{2}{6} = \frac{1}{3}$.

Note that the probability of having the die come up either 4 or 5 (1/3) is greater than the probability of a 4 by itself (1/6) or of a 5 by itself (1/6). This should make intuitive sense. If you define success in a less constrained way (e.g., "I can win EITHER this way OR that way"), then the probability of success will be higher. The operation of addition should also make sense. Typical probabilities are fractions between 0 and 1. When you add together two such fractions, you make a *larger* product.

Of course, not all "OR" problems will actually contain the word "or". Instead, you will see some "OR in disguise" problems. Such problems ask for the probability of what *seems* to be a single event, but in fact is a collection of separate events whose probabilities must be added together. Consider the following problem:

> Molly is playing a game that requires her to roll a fair die repeatedly until she first rolls a 1, at which point she must stop rolling the die. What is the probability that Molly will roll the die less than four times before stopping?

The simple wording of this problem hides two levels of complexity. First, "less than four times" sounds like a single event, but it actually includes three different events: one roll, two rolls, or three rolls. Furthermore, two of these three events are actually series of events. "Two rolls" means that Molly must not roll a 1 on her first roll, but she must do so on her second roll. "Three rolls" means that she must avoid a 1 on her first two rolls and then produce a 1 on her third. Therefore, the total probability is

$$P(\text{one roll}) + P(\text{two rolls}) + P(\text{three rolls}) = \frac{1}{6} + \left(\frac{5}{6} \cdot \frac{1}{6}\right) + \left(\frac{5}{6} \cdot \frac{5}{6} \cdot \frac{1}{6}\right) = \frac{91}{216}$$

You should handle "OR" problems in one of two ways, depending on whether the events can occur together in the same scenario.

If an "OR" problem features events that **<u>cannot</u> occur together**, then you can find the "OR" probability by **adding** the probabilities of the individual events, as illustrated above.

If an "OR" problem features events that **<u>can</u> occur together**, then use the following **formula** to find the "OR" probability:

$$P(A \text{ **or** } B) = P(A) + P(B) - P(A \text{ **and** } B)$$

OR means add the probabilities. You will wind up with a larger number, which indicates a larger probability of success.

If you simply add $P(A)$ and $P(B)$ in situations when A and B can occur together, then you are overestimating the probability of either A or B (or both) occurring. You would be making the same error if you said that because you have a 50% chance of getting heads on one coin flip, you simply double that chance to 100% for *two* coin flips. But you will not *always* get heads at least once in two coin flips. What you have to do is subtract the chance of getting heads on both flips, because the event $H1$ ("heads on first flip") CAN occur together in the same scenario with event $H2$ ("heads on second flip"). In other words, you CAN get two heads in a row, so you must subtract that possibility in the formula.

$$P(H1 \text{ or } H2) = P(H1) + P(H2) - P(H1 \text{ and } H2)$$
$$= 1/2 \quad + 1/2 \quad - (1/2)(1/2)$$
$$= 3/4$$

In the OR formula, remember to subtract the probability that both events occur together.

3/4 or 75% is the true chance of getting heads at least once in two fair coin flips.

This formula actually works for all "OR" problems. However, it is a waste of time for problems in which events A and B cannot occur together, because then the right-hand term is zero. In such cases, you can simply write $P(A \text{ or } B) = P(A) + P(B)$.

> A fair die is rolled once and a fair coin is flipped once. What is the probability that either the die will land on 3 or that the coin will land on heads?

These outcomes are not mutually exclusive, since both can occur together. The probability that the die will land on 3 is 1/6. The probability that the coin will land on heads is 1/2.

The probability of both these events occurring is $\dfrac{1}{6} \times \dfrac{1}{2} = \dfrac{1}{12}$.

Therefore, the probability of either event occurring is $\left(\dfrac{1}{6} + \dfrac{1}{2} \right) - \dfrac{1}{12} = \dfrac{7}{12}$.

The $1 - x$ Probability Trick

As shown on the previous page, you can solve "OR" problems (explicit or disguised) by combining the probabilities of individual events. If there are many individual events, though, such calculation may be tedious and time-consuming. The good news is that you may not have to perform these calculations. In certain types of "OR" problems, the probability of the desired event NOT happening may be much easier to calculate.

For example, in the previous section, we could have calculated the probability of getting at least one head on two flips by considering how we would NOT get at least one head. However, it was not too much work to compute the probability directly, using the slightly more complicated "OR" formula.

But let us say that a salesperson makes five sales calls, and you want to find the likelihood that he or she makes *at least one* sale. If you try to calculate this probability directly, you will have to confront five separate possibilities that constitute "success": exactly 1 sale, exactly 2 sales, exactly 3 sales, exactly 4 sales, or exactly 5 sales. You would have no choice but to calculate each of those probabilities separately and then add them together. This will be far too much work, especially under timed conditions.

However, consider the probability of *failure*—that is, the salesperson *does not* make at least one sale. Now you have only one possibility to consider: zero sales. You can now calculate the probability in which you are interested, because for *any* event, the following relationship is true:

Probability of SUCCESS + Probability of FAILURE = 1
(the event happens)   (it does not happen)

*If on a GMAT problem, "success" contains **multiple possibilities**—especially if the wording contains phrases such as **"at least"** and **"at most"**—then consider finding the probability that success **does not happen**. If you can find this "failure" probability more easily (call it x), then the probability you really want to find will be **1 − x**.*

For example:

> What is the probability that, on three rolls of a single fair die, AT LEAST ONE of the rolls will be a six?

We could list all the possible outcomes of three rolls of a die (1–1–1, 1–1–2, 1–1–3, etc.), and then determine how many of them have at least one six, but this would be very time-consuming. Instead, it is easier to think of this problem in reverse before solving.

> Failure: What is the probability that NONE of the rolls will yield a 6?

On each roll, there is a $\frac{5}{6}$ probability that the die will not yield a 6.

Thus, the probability that on all 3 rolls the die will not yield a 6 is $\frac{5}{6} \times \frac{5}{6} \times \frac{5}{6} = \frac{125}{216}$.

Now, we originally defined success as rolling at least one six. Since we have found the probability of failure, we answer the original question by subtracting this probability from 1:

$$1 - \frac{125}{216} = \frac{91}{216}$$ is the probability that at least one six will be rolled.

The Domino Effect

Sometimes the outcome of the first event will affect the probability of a subsequent event. For example:

> In a box with 10 blocks, 3 of which are red, what is the probability of picking out a red block on each of your first two tries? Assume that you do not replace the first block after you have picked it.

Since this is an "AND" problem, we must find the probability of both events and multiply them together. Consider how easy it is to make the following mistake:

You compute the probability of picking a red block on your first pick as $\frac{3}{10}$.

*Manhattan*GMAT*Prep
the new standard

Sometimes it is easier to calculate the probability that an event will NOT happen than the probability that the event WILL happen.

You compute the probability of picking a red block on your second pick as $\frac{3}{10}$.

So you compute the probability of picking a red block on both picks as $\frac{3}{10} \times \frac{3}{10} = \frac{9}{100}$.

This solution is WRONG, because it does not take into account that the first event affects the second event. If a red block is chosen on the first pick, then the number of blocks now in the box has decreased from **10 to 9**. Additionally, the number of red blocks now in the box has decreased from **3 to 2**. Therefore, the probability of choosing a red block on the second pick is different from the probability of choosing a red block on the first pick.

The CORRECT solution to this problem is as follows:

The probability of picking a red block on your first pick is $\frac{3}{10}$.

The probability of picking a red block on your second pick is $\frac{2}{9}$.

Therefore, the probability of picking a red block on both picks is $\frac{3}{10} \times \frac{2}{9} = \frac{6}{90} = \frac{1}{15}$.

Do not forget to analyze events by considering whether one event affects subsequent events. The first roll of a die or flip of a coin has no affect on any subsequent rolls or flips. However, the first pick of an object out of a box does affect subsequent picks if you do not replace that object. This scenario is called "without replacement."

If you <u>are</u> supposed to replace the object, the problem should clearly tell you so. In this scenario (called "with replacement"), the first pick does not affect the second pick.

Probability Trees

Trees can be a useful tool to keep track of branching possibilities and "winning scenarios." Consider the following problem:

> Renee has a bag of 6 candies, 4 of which are sweet and 2 of which are sour. Jack picks two candies simultaneously and at random. What is the chance that exactly 1 of the candies he has picked is sour?

Even though Jack picks the two candies simultaneously, you can pretend that he picks them in a sequence. This trick allows you to set up a tree reflecting Jack's picks at each stage.

The tree is shown at the top of the next page. Label each branch and put in probabilities. Jack has a 2/6 chance of picking a sour candy first and a 4/6 chance of picking a sweet candy first. Note that these probabilities add to 1. On the second set of branches, put the probabilities AS IF Jack has already made his first pick. Remember The Domino Effect! Notice also that the probabilities in the lower branches are different from those in the upper branches. The first pick affects the second pick.

Be careful of situations in which the outcome of the first event affects the probability of the second event.

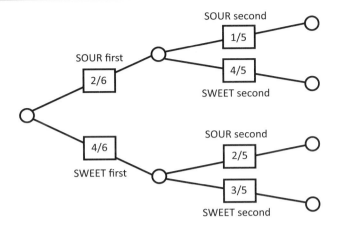

Now compute the probabilities of the WINNING SCENARIOS. One scenario is "sour first" AND "sweet second"; the other is "sweet first" AND "sour second." Since each scenario is one event AND another event occurring together, you MULTIPLY the basic probabilities. In other words, you "multiply the branches":

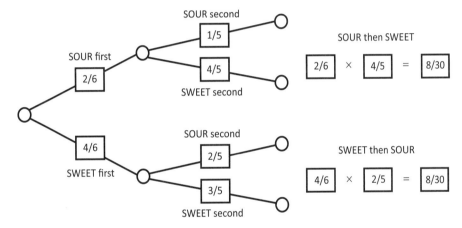

Finally, EITHER one scenario OR the other scenario works: in either case, Jack picks exactly one sour candy. So you ADD these probabilities: 8/30 + 8/30 = 16/30 = 8/15. In other words, you "add the leaves" of the winning scenarios.

Avoid setting up complicated trees, which GMAT problems almost never require. Instead, use trees to conceptualize a path through the problem.

Combinatorics and Probability (Advanced)

In some difficult probability problems, both the "desired" possibilities and the total possibilities require complex organized counting. In such problems, do not be afraid to **use combinatorial methods**, as described in the previous chapter, **to calculate the numbers of possibilities.** Once you have those numbers, set up the probability as a fraction, as always.

> Kate and her twin sister Amy want to be on the same relay-race team. There are 6 girls in the group, and only 4 of them will be placed at random on the team. What is the probability that Kate and Amy will both be on the team?

When you use a probability tree, multiply down the branches and add across the results.

The winning scenario method, discussed in the previous section, involves finding the probability of each winning scenario. The 12 winning scenarios are shown to the right. The next step in this method would be to calculate the probability of each winning scenario and then to add all the probabilities.

Pick (1)	Pick (2)	Pick (3)	Pick (4)
Kate	Amy	X	X
Amy	Kate	X	X
X	Kate	Amy	X
X	Amy	Kate	X
X	X	Kate	Amy
X	X	Amy	Kate
Kate	X	X	Amy
Amy	X	X	Kate
Kate	X	Amy	X
Amy	X	Kate	X
X	Kate	X	Amy
X	Amy	X	Kate

Use counting methods to find the total number of possibilities.

As you can see, this method would be tedious in this problem. Instead, we can solve this problem using the counting methods described in the section on combinatorics. Create an *Anagram Grid* to find the number of different 4-person teams:

A	B	C	D	E	F
Y	Y	Y	Y	N	N

There are $\dfrac{6!}{4!2!}$ = 15 different teams.

Each of the winning scenarios will include Kate and Amy, plus 2 of the remaining 4 girls. Therefore, we *Reduce the Pool* by 2 people, and we find the number of winning scenarios by counting the ways we can choose 2 of the remaining 4 girls:

A	B	C	D
Y	Y	N	N

There are $\dfrac{4!}{2!2!}$ = 6 winning scenarios.

Alternately, you can list the winning teams:

Kate, Amy, A, B	Kate, Amy, B, C
Kate, Amy, A, C	Kate, Amy, B, D
Kate, Amy, A, D	Kate, Amy, C, D

Therefore, the probability is 6/15, or 2/5.

Combinatorics and The Domino Effect (Advanced)

The domino-effect rule states that you multiply the probabilities of events in a sequence, taking earlier events into account. This is generally straightforward. Some domino-effect problems are difficult because of the sheer number of possibilities involved. When all possibilities are equivalent, though, combinatorics can save the day. Consider the following:

> A miniature gumball machine contains 7 blue, 5 green, and 4 red gumballs, which are identical except for their colors. If the machine dispenses three gumballs at random, what is the probability that it dispenses one gumball of each color?

Consider one specific case: blue first, then green, then red. By the domino-effect rule, the

probability of this case is $\dfrac{7\,\text{blue}}{16\,\text{total}} \times \dfrac{5\,\text{green}}{15\,\text{total}} \times \dfrac{4\,\text{red}}{14\,\text{total}} = \dfrac{\cancel{7}}{\cancel{16}\,4} \times \dfrac{\cancel{5}}{\cancel{15}\,3} \times \dfrac{\cancel{4}}{\cancel{14}\,2} = \dfrac{1}{24}$.

Now consider another case: green first, then red, then blue. The probability of this case is

$\dfrac{5\,\text{green}}{16\,\text{total}} \times \dfrac{4\,\text{red}}{15\,\text{total}} \times \dfrac{7\,\text{blue}}{14\,\text{total}} = \dfrac{\cancel{5}}{\cancel{16}\,4} \times \dfrac{\cancel{4}}{\cancel{15}\,3} \times \dfrac{\cancel{7}}{\cancel{14}\,2} = \dfrac{1}{24}$. Notice that all we have done is

swap around the numerators. *We get the same final probability!* This is no accident; the order
in which the balls come out does not matter.

Because the three desired gumballs can come out in any order, there are 3! = 6 different
cases. *All of these cases must have the same probability.* Therefore, the overall probability is

$6 \times \dfrac{1}{24} = \dfrac{1}{4}$.

In general, when you have a symmetrical problem with multiple equivalent cases, calculate
the probability of one case (often by using the domino-effect rule). Then multiply by the
number of cases. Use combinatorics to calculate the number of cases, if necessary.

Remember that when you apply a symmetry argument, the situation must truly be symmetrical. In the case above, if you swapped the order of "red" and "green" emerging from the
gumball machine, nothing would change about the problem. As a result, we can use symmetry to simplify the computation.

Reformulating Difficult Problems (Advanced)

Some GMAT probability problems are not as complicated as they outwardly appear. Earlier
in this chapter, you saw that "at least" and "at most" problems can be solved much more
quickly and easily with the 1 − *x* approach. More generally, many problems for which the
direct approach is tedious and time-consuming can be creatively *reformulated* so they are
easier to solve. Your goal is to reduce the number or complexity of calculations.

*If a probability problem seems to require extensive calculation, try to reformulate it in a way that
either **takes advantage of symmetry** in the problem or **groups several individual cases
together** at once.*

Two examples follow.

> A medical researcher must choose one of 14 patients to receive an experi-
> mental medicine called Progaine. The researcher must then choose one of
> the remaining 13 patients to receive another medicine, called Ropecia.
> Finally, the researcher administers a placebo to one of the remaining 12
> patients. All choices are equally random. If Donald is one of the 14 patients,
> what is the probability that Donald receives either Progaine or Ropecia?

Use the idea of symmetry
to simplify cases or
reduce their number in
difficult problems.

*Manhattan*GMAT*Prep
the new standard

The "textbook" approach to this problem—finding the total number of different distributions giving either Progaine or Ropecia to Donald, and then dividing that number by the total number of distributions—can be time-consuming. Instead, notice the *symmetry* of the problem. None of the 14 patients is "special" in any way, so *each of them must have the same chance* of receiving Progaine or Ropecia. Since Progaine is only administered to one patient, each patient (including Donald) must have probability 1/14 of receiving it. The same logic also holds for Ropecia. Since Donald cannot receive both of the medicines, the desired probability is the probability of receiving Progaine, plus the probability of receiving Ropecia: 1/14 + 1/14 = 1/7.

The placebo is irrelevant, as is the order that the researcher artificially chose for the selection process. You *can* solve this problem by using a sequence of two choices (Progaine or not; if not, then Ropecia or not). But it is faster to use a symmetry argument.

> A gambler rolls three fair six-sided dice. What is the probability that two of the dice show the same number, but the third shows a different number?

The textbook approach to this problem would be formidable. You would have to work out the total number of combinations of two of one number and one of another *and* figure out the different orders in which those numbers could appear on the dice. Instead, you can formulate possibilities that encompass many cases at once, if you do *not* specify the actual numbers that turn up on the dice. Let the result of the first die be *any number*—so that you do not need to include the first die in the probability calculation—and concentrate on whether the second and third dice *match* the first die. There are only three possibilities:

- Second matches first, third does not: $\dfrac{1}{6} \times \dfrac{5}{6} = \dfrac{5}{36}$

- Third matches first, second does not: $\dfrac{5}{6} \times \dfrac{1}{6} = \dfrac{5}{36}$

- Second and third match each other: $\dfrac{5}{6} \times \dfrac{1}{6} = \dfrac{5}{36}$

In the last case, the second die's probability is 5/6 because the die can show any number *other* than the number showing on the first die. The third probability is only 1/6 because the third die must match the second one. The total probability is therefore 15/36.

Alternatively, we can bring in the idea of symmetry. Imagine that we color the dice red, green and blue, and then roll them all at once. Also imagine that the red and green dice come up the same number, whereas the blue die comes up a different number. The probability of this occurrence ("blue die is different") is $1 \times \dfrac{1}{6} \times \dfrac{5}{6} = \dfrac{5}{36}$, as above. However, the "different numbered" die could have been any one of the three dice, with equal likelihood. The event "one die is different" is composed of three symmetrical events: "blue die is different," "red die is different," and "green die is different." The colors do not really matter, so the probability of "one die is different" is simply $3 \times \dfrac{5}{36} = \dfrac{15}{36}$.

By reconceptualizing winning cases, you can often group many of them together.

Problem Set

Solve the following problems. Express probabilities as fractions or percentages unless otherwise instructed.

1. What is the probability that the sum of two dice will yield a 4 or 6?

2. What is the probability that the sum of two dice will yield anything but an 8?

3. What is the probability that the sum of two dice will yield a 10 or lower?

4. What is the probability that the sum of two dice will yield a 7, and then when both are thrown again, their sum will again yield a 7?

5. What is the probability that the sum of two dice will yield a 5, and then when both are thrown again, their sum will yield a 9?

6. There is a 30% chance of rain and a 70% chance of shine. If it rains, there is a 50% chance that Bob will cancel his picnic, but if the sun is shining, he will definitely have his picnic. What is the chance that Bob will have his picnic?

7. At a certain pizzeria, 1/6 of the pizzas sold in a week were cheese, and 1/5 of the OTHER pizzas sold were pepperoni. If Brandon bought a randomly chosen pizza from the pizzeria that week, what is the probability that he ordered a pepperoni?

8. In a diving competition, each diver has a 20% chance of a perfect dive. The first perfect dive of the competition, but no subsequent dives, will receive a perfect score. If Janet is the third diver to dive, what is her chance of receiving a perfect score? (Express your answer as a percentage.)

9. In a bag of marbles, there are 3 red, 2 white, and 5 blue. If Bob takes 2 marbles out of the bag, what is the probability that he will have one white and one blue marble?

10. A florist has 2 azaleas, 3 buttercups, and 4 petunias. She puts two flowers together at random in a bouquet. However, the customer calls and says that she does not want two of the same flower. What is the probability that the florist does not have to change the bouquet?

11. Five A-list actresses are vying for the three leading roles in the new film, "Catfight in Denmark." The actresses are Julia Robards, Meryl Strep, Sally Fieldstone, Lauren Bake-all, and Hallie Strawberry. Assuming that no actress has any advantage in getting any role, what is the probability that Julia and Hallie will star in the film together?

12. A polling company reports that there is a 40% chance that a certain candidate will win the next election. If the candidate wins, there is a 60% chance that she will sign Bill X and no other bills. If she decides not to sign Bill X, she will sign either Bill Y or Bill Z, chosen randomly. What is the chance that the candidate will sign Bill Z?

13. A magician has five animals in his magic hat: 3 doves and 2 rabbits. If he pulls two animals out of the hat at random, what is the chance that he will have a matched pair?

14. If Lauren, Mary, Nancy, Oprah, and Penny sit randomly in a row, what is the probability that Oprah and Penny are NOT next to each other?

15. Kevin has wired 6 light bulbs to a board so that, when he presses a button, each bulb has an equal chance of lighting up or staying dark. Each of the six bulbs is independent of the other five.

     (a) In how many different configurations could the bulbs on the board light up (including the configuration in which *none* of them light up)?

     (b) In how many configurations could exactly three of the bulbs light up?

     (c) When Kevin presses the button, what is the probability that exactly three of the bulbs light up?

16. (Very difficult!) A lottery game works as follows: The player draws a numbered ball at random from an urn containing five balls numbered 1, 2, 3, 4, and 5. If the number on the ball is even, the player loses the game and receives no points; if the number on the ball is odd, the player receives the number of points indicated on the ball. Afterward, he or she replaces the ball in the urn and draws again. On each subsequent turn, the player loses the game if the *total* of all the numbers drawn becomes even, and gets another turn (after receiving the number of points indicated on the ball and then replacing the ball in the urn) each time the total remains odd.

     (a) What is the probability that the player loses the game on the third turn?

     (b) What is the probability that the player accumulates exactly 7 points and then loses on the next turn?

1. **2/9:** : There are 36 ways in which 2 dice can be thrown (6 × 6 = 36). The combinations that yield sums of 4 and 6 are 1 + 3, 2 + 2, 3 + 1, 1 + 5, 2 + 4, 3 + 3, 4 + 2, and 5 + 1: 8 different combinations. Therefore, the probability is 8/36, or 2/9.

2. **31/36:** Solve this problem by calculating the probability that the sum WILL yield a sum of 8, and then subtract the result from 1. There are 5 combinations of 2 dice that yield a sum of 8: 2 + 6, 3 + 5, 4 + 4, 5 + 3, and 6 + 2. (Note that 7 + 1 is not a valid combination, as there is no 7 on a standard die.) Therefore, the probability that the sum will be 8 is 5/36, and the probability that the sum will NOT be 8 is 1 − 5/36, or 31/36.

3. **11/12:** Solve this problem by calculating the probability that the sum will be higher than 10, and subtract the result from 1. There are 3 combinations of 2 dice that yield a sum higher than 10: 5 + 6, 6 + 5, and 6 + 6. Therefore, the probability that the sum will be higher than 10 is 3/36, or 1/12. The probability that the sum will be 10 or lower is 1 − 1/12 = 11/12.

4. **1/36:** There are 36 ways in which 2 dice can be thrown (6 × 6 = 36). The combinations that yield a sum of 7 are 1 + 6, 2 + 5, 3 + 4, 4 + 3, 5 + 2, and 6 + 1: 6 different combinations. Therefore, the probability of rolling a 7 is 6/36, or 1/6. To find the probability that this will happen twice in a row, multiply 1/6 by 1/6 to get 1/36.

5. **1/81:** First, find the individual probability of each event. The probability of rolling a 5 is 4/36, or 1/9, since there are 4 ways to roll a sum of 5 (1 + 4, 2 + 3, 3 + 2, and 4 + 1). The probability of rolling a 9 is also 4/36, or 1/9, since there are 4 ways to roll a sum of 9 (3 + 6, 4 + 5, 5 + 4, and 6 + 3). To find the probability that both events will happen in succession, multiply 1/9 × 1/9: 1/81.

6. **85%:** There are two possible chains of events in which Bob will have the picnic:

One: The sun shines: P = 7/10 = 14/20   **OR**
Two: It rains AND Bob chooses to have the picnic anyway: P = (3/10)(1/2) = 3/20

Add the probabilities together to find the total probability that Bob will have the picnic:
14/20 + 3/20 = 17/20 = 85%

7. **1/6:** If 1/6 of the pizzas were cheese, 5/6 of the pizzas were not. 1/5 of these 5/6 were pepperoni. Multiply to find the total portion: 1/5 × 5/6 = 1/6. If 1/6 of the pizzas were pepperoni, there is a 1/6 chance that Brandon bought a pepperoni pizza.

8. **12.8%:** In order for Janet to receive a perfect score, neither of the previous two divers can receive one. Therefore, we are finding the probability of a chain of three events: that diver one will <u>not</u> get a perfect score AND diver two will <u>not</u> get a perfect score AND Janet <u>will</u> get a perfect score. Multiply the probabilities: 8/10 × 8/10 × 2/10 = 128/1000 = 12.8%

There is a 12.8% chance that Janet will receive a perfect score.

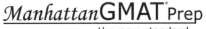

9. **2/9:** You can solve this problem by listing the winning scenarios or by using combinatorics counting methods. Both solutions are presented below:

(1) LIST THE WINNING SCENARIOS.

First Pick	Second Pick	Probability
(1) Blue (1/2)	White (2/9)	$1/2 \times 2/9 = 1/9$
(2) White (1/5)	Blue (5/9)	$1/5 \times 5/9 = 1/9$

To find the probability, add the probabilities of the winning scenarios: $1/9 + 1/9 = 2/9$.

(2) USE THE COUNTING METHOD.

A	B	C	D	E	F	G	H	I	J
Y	Y	N	N	N	N	N	N	N	N

There are $\dfrac{10!}{2!8!} = 45$ different combinations of marbles.

Since there are 2 white marbles and 5 blue marbles, there are $2 \times 5 = 10$ different white–blue combinations. Therefore, the probability of selecting a blue and white combination is 10/45, or 2/9.

10. **13/18:** Solve this problem by finding the probability that the two flowers in the bouquet WILL be the same, and then subtract the result from 1. The table to the right indicates that there are 10 different bouquets in which both flowers are the same. Then, find the number of different 2-flower bouquets that can be made in total, using an anagram model. In how many different ways can you arrange the letters in the "word" YYNNNNNNN?

$$\frac{9!}{7!2!} = \frac{9 \times 8}{2 \times 1} = 36$$

Flower #1	Flower #2
A_1	A_2
B_1	B_2
B_1	B_3
B_2	B_3
P_1	P_2
P_1	P_3
P_1	P_4
P_2	P_3
P_2	P_4
P_3	P_4

The probability of randomly putting together a bouquet that contains two of the same type of flower is 10/36, or 5/18. Therefore, the probability of randomly putting together a bouquet that contains two different flowers and that therefore will NOT need to be changed is $1 - 5/18$, or 13/18.

11. **3/10:** The probability of Julia being cast first is 1/5. If Julia is cast, the probability of Hallie being cast second is 1/4. The probability of any of the remaining 3 actresses being cast is 3/3, or 1. Therefore, the probability of this chain of events is:

$$1/5 \times 1/4 \times 1 = 1/20$$

There are six event chains that yield this outcome, shown in the chart to the right. Therefore, the total probability that Julia and Hallie will be among the 3 leading actresses is:

$$1/20 \times 6 = 6/20 = 3/10$$

Actress (1)	Actress (2)	Actress (3)
Julia	Hallie	X
Julia	X	Hallie
Hallie	Julia	X
Hallie	X	Julia
X	Julia	Hallie
X	Hallie	Julia

Alternately, you can solve this problem with counting methods.

The number of different combinations in which the actresses can be cast in the roles, assuming we are not concerned with which actress is given which role, is $\dfrac{5!}{3!2!} = 10$.

A	B	C	D	E
Y	Y	N	N	N

There are 3 possible combinations that feature both Julia and Hallie: (1) Julia, Hallie, Sally
(2) Julia, Hallie, Meryl
(3) Julia, Hallie, Lauren

Therefore, the probability that Julia and Hallie will star together is $\dfrac{3}{10}$.

12. **8%:** In order for the candidate to sign Bill Z, the following chain of events would need to take place:

    (1) She would have to win the election.
    (2) She would have to decide not to sign Bill X.
    (3) She would have to decide to sign Bill Z.

Assign each independent event a probability:

    (1) There is a 40% chance that she will win the election   AND
    (2) There is a 40% chance that she will not sign Bill X   AND
    (3) There is a 50% chance that she will sign Bill Z.

Multiply the probabilities of each event to find the probability that the entire event chain will occur:

$$\frac{4}{10} \times \frac{4}{10} \times \frac{5}{10} = \frac{80}{1000} = 8\%$$

There is an 8% chance that the candidate will sign Bill Z.

13. **40%:** Use an anagram model to find out the total number of different pairs the magician can pull out of his hat. Since two animals will be in the pair and the other three will not, use the "word" YYNNN.

A	B	C	D	E
Y	Y	N	N	N

$\dfrac{5!}{2!3!} = \dfrac{5 \times 4}{2 \times 1} = 10$ There are 10 possible pairs.

Then, list the pairs in which the animals will match. Represent the rabbits with the letters A and B, and the doves with the letters X, Y, and Z.

Matched Pairs: R_aR_b D_xD_y There are four pairs in which the animals
                    D_xD_z D_yD_z will be a matched set.

Therefore, the probability that the magician will randomly draw a matched set is $\dfrac{4}{10} = 40\%$.

*Manhattan*GMAT*Prep

14. **3/5:** Use counting methods to find the total number of ways in which the five girls can sit.

A	B	C	D	E
1	2	3	4	5

There are 5! = 120 ways in which the five girls can sit.

It is simpler to find the arrangements in which Oprah and Penny ARE next to each other than the ones in which they are NOT next to each other.

OPXXX	XOPXX	XXOPX	XXXOP
POXXX	XPOXX	XXPOX	XXXPO

There are 8 arrangements in which Oprah and Penny are next to each other. For each of these arrangements, there are 3! = 6 ways in which the three other girls can be arranged.

$$6 \times 8 = 48$$

Therefore, the probability that Oprah and Penny WILL sit next to each other is $\dfrac{48}{120}$, or $\dfrac{2}{5}$.

The probability that Oprah and Penny will NOT sit next to each other is $1 - \dfrac{2}{5} = \dfrac{3}{5}$.

15. (a) **64:** For each bulb, there are two options: on and off. Since all of the bulbs are independent, we can multiply these numbers of possibilities together: $2 \times 2 \times 2 \times 2 \times 2 \times 2 = 64$.

(b) **20:** There are three "on", or "yes", bulbs and three "off", or "no", bulbs, so this problem is equivalent to finding the number of anagrams of the "word" YYYNNN. This is $\dfrac{6!}{(3!)(3!)} = 20$ ways.

You could also make an organized list of the twenty different ways of choosing three bulbs, using alphabetical order: *ABC, ABD, ABE, ABF, ACD, ACE, ACF, ADE, ADF, AEF, BCD, BCE, BCF, BDE, BDF, BEF, CDE, CDF, CEF, DEF.*

(c) **5/16:** Since the bulbs are just as likely to light up as to go dark, and are independent of one another, each possible configuration of the bulbs has the same probability. Therefore, the desired probability is

$$\frac{\text{configurations with 3 bulbs on}}{\text{total configurations}} = \frac{20}{64} = \frac{5}{16}.$$

16. Perhaps the most difficult aspect of this problem is to understand the rules of the game and to set up scenarios properly. Recall that *odd + even = odd* and that *odd + odd = even*. Therefore, to **stay in** the game, the player must select an **odd**-numbered ball on the **first** draw, and an **even**-numbered ball on **each subsequent** draw (so that the sum remains odd).

Since we are replacing the ball each time, the outcomes of any single draw, at any stage of the game, have constant probabilities that are straightforward to compute:

The probability of drawing any specific number = 1/5.
The probability of drawing an **even** number = 2/5 (since the set contains two even numbers: 2 and 4).
The probability of drawing an **odd** number = 3/5 (since the set contains three odd numbers: 1, 3, and 5).

Moreover, since each draw is independent of every other draw, you multiply the probabilities at each stage to compute the probability of any sequence of draws.

(a) To lose the game on the third turn, the player must draw an odd number on the first turn, an even number on the second turn, and an odd number on the third turn. The probability of this event is

$$\left(\frac{3}{5}\right)\left(\frac{2}{5}\right)\left(\frac{3}{5}\right) = \frac{18}{125}.$$

(b) Find all of the different ways in which the player can attain 7 points and <u>then</u> lose. Generate each of the sequences by following the constraints of the game (odd number first, then only even numbers).

* 1, 2, 2, 2, odd number: $\left(\frac{1}{5}\right)\left(\frac{1}{5}\right)\left(\frac{1}{5}\right)\left(\frac{1}{5}\right)\left(\frac{3}{5}\right) = \frac{3}{3,125}$

* 1, 2, 4, odd number: $\left(\frac{1}{5}\right)\left(\frac{1}{5}\right)\left(\frac{1}{5}\right)\left(\frac{3}{5}\right) = \frac{3}{625} = \frac{15}{3,125}$

* 1, 4, 2, odd number: $\left(\frac{1}{5}\right)\left(\frac{1}{5}\right)\left(\frac{1}{5}\right)\left(\frac{3}{5}\right) = \frac{3}{625} = \frac{15}{3,125}$

* 3, 2, 2, odd number: $\left(\frac{1}{5}\right)\left(\frac{1}{5}\right)\left(\frac{1}{5}\right)\left(\frac{3}{5}\right) = \frac{3}{625} = \frac{15}{3,125}$

* 3, 4, odd number: $\left(\frac{1}{5}\right)\left(\frac{1}{5}\right)\left(\frac{3}{5}\right) = \frac{3}{125} = \frac{75}{3,125}$

* 5, 2, odd number: $\left(\frac{1}{5}\right)\left(\frac{1}{5}\right)\left(\frac{3}{5}\right) = \frac{3}{125} = \frac{75}{3,125}$

The total of all these probabilities is $\frac{198}{3,125}$.

Chapter 6
of
WORD TRANSLATIONS

STATISTICS

In This Chapter . . .

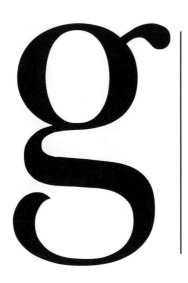

- Averages

- Using the Average Formula

- Evenly Spaced Sets: Take the Middle

- Weighted Averages

- Median: The Middle Number

- Standard Deviation

- Two Time-Saving Shortcuts for Averages (Advanced)

AVERAGES

The average (or the arithmetic mean) of a set is given by the following formula:

$$\text{Average} = \frac{\text{Sum}}{\text{\# of terms}}, \text{ which is abbreviated as } A = \frac{S}{n}.$$

The sum, S, refers to the sum of all the terms in the set.
The number, n, refers to the number of terms that are in the set.
The average, A, refers to the average value (arithmetic mean) of the terms in the set.

A commonly used variation of the above formula is this:

$$(\text{Average}) \times (\text{\# of terms}) = (\text{Sum}), \text{ or } A \cdot n = S.$$

This formula has the same basic form as the RT = D equation, so it lends itself readily to the same kind of table you would use for RTD problems.

Every GMAT problem dealing with averages can be solved with one of these two formulas. In general, if the average is unknown, the first formula (the definition of average) will solve the problem more directly. If the average is known, the second formula is better.

In any case, if you are asked to use or find the average of a set, you should not concentrate on the individual terms of the set. As you can see from the formulas above, all that matters is the *sum* of the terms—which can often be found even if the individual terms cannot be determined.

In many average problems, only the SUM is important.

Using the Average Formula

The first thing to do for any GMAT average problem is to write down the average formula. Then, fill in any of the 3 variables (S, n, and A) that are given in the problem.

> The sum of 6 numbers is 90. What is the average term?

$$A = \frac{S}{n}$$

The sum, S, is given as 90. The number of terms, n, is given as 6. By plugging in, we can solve for the average: $\frac{90}{6} = 15$.

Notice that you do NOT need to know each term in the set to find the average!

Sometimes, using the average formula will be more involved. For example:

> If the average of the set {2, 5, 5, 7, 8, 9, x} is 6.1, what is the value of x?

Plug the given information into the average formula, and solve for x.

$$A \cdot n = S$$

$$(6.1)(7 \text{ terms}) = 2 + 5 + 5 + 7 + 8 + 9 + x$$
$$42.7 = 36 + x$$
$$6.7 = x$$

More complex average problems involve setting up two average formulas. For example:

> Sam earned a $2,000 commission on a big sale, raising his average commission by $100. If Sam's new average commission is $900, how many sales has he made?

To keep track of two average formulas in the same problem, you can set up an *RTD*-style table. Instead of $RT = D$, we use $A \cdot n = S$, which has the same form.

Note that the Number and Sum columns add up to give the new cumulative values, but the values in the Average column do *not* add up:

	Average	×	Number	=	Sum
Old Total	800	×	n	=	$800n$
This Sale	2000	×	1	=	2000
New Total	900	×	$n + 1$	=	$900(n + 1)$

The right-hand column gives the equation we need:

$$800n + 2000 = 900(n + 1)$$
$$800n + 2000 = 900n + 900$$
$$1100 = 100n$$
$$11 = n$$

Since we are looking for the new number of sales, which is $n + 1$, Sam has made a total of 12 sales.

Evenly Spaced Sets: Take the Middle

You may recall that the average of a set of consecutive integers is the middle number. This is true for any set in which the terms are spaced evenly apart. For example:

The average of the set {3, 5, 7, 9, 11} is the middle term 7, because all the terms in the set are spaced evenly apart (in this case, they are spaced 2 units apart).

The average of the set {12, 20, 28, 36, 44, 52, 60, 68, 76} is the middle term 44, because all the terms in the set are spaced evenly apart (in this case, they are spaced 8 units apart).

Note that if an evenly spaced set has two "middle" numbers, the average of the set is the average of these two middle numbers. For example:

The average of the set {5, 10, 15, 20, 25, 30} is 17.5, because this is the average of the two middle numbers, 15 and 20.

You do not have to write out each term of an evenly spaced set to find the middle number—the average term. All you need to do to find the middle number is to add the **first** and **last** terms and divide that sum by 2. For example:

The average of the set {101, 111, 121…581, 591, 601} is equal to 351, which is the sum of the first and last terms (101 + 601 = 702) divided by 2.

To find the average of an evenly spaced set, simply take the middle number in the set.

Weighted Averages

The basic formula for averages applies only to sets of data consisting of individual values, all of which are equally weighted (i.e., none of the values "counts" toward the average any more than any other value does).

When you consider sets in which some data are more heavily weighted than other data—whether weighted by percents, frequencies, ratios, or fractions—you need to use special techniques for *weighted averages*.

For instance, consider the following problem:

> In a translation class, 40% of a student's grade comes from exam perform-ance, 30% from written assignments, 20% from conversational practice, and 10% from simultaneous interpretation. If a student's grades are 94 for exams, 88 for written assignments, 98 for conversational practice, and 85 for simultaneous interpretation, what is the student's overall grade in the course?

You cannot solve this problem by merely adding 94, 88, 98, and 85 and then dividing by four, because the four data points do not have equal weight. Instead, use the following formula, which applies to all weighted averages:

$$\text{Weighted average} = \frac{(\text{data point})(\text{weight}) + (\text{data point})(\text{weight}) + \cdots + (\text{data point})(\text{weight})}{\text{sum of weights}}$$

Applied to the problem above, this formula gives

$$\text{Weighted average} = \frac{(94)(0.4) + (88)(0.3) + (98)(0.2) + (85)(0.1)}{0.4 + 0.3 + 0.2 + 0.1} = \frac{92.1}{1} = 92.1$$

If the "weights" are fractions or percentages, as in the problem above, then the denominator of the weighted-average expression (*sum of weights*) will be 1.

Properties of Weighted Averages

Although weighted averages differ from traditional averages, they are still averages—meaning that their values will still fall *between* the values being averaged (or between the highest and lowest of those values, if there are more than two).

A weighted average of only *two* values will fall closer to whichever value is weighted more heavily. For instance, if a drink is made by mixing 2 shots of a liquor containing 15% alcohol with 3 shots of a liquor containing 20% alcohol, then the alcohol content of the mixed drink will be closer to 20% than to 15%.

Finally—and importantly, especially for data sufficiency problems—you do not necessarily need concrete values for the weights in a weighted-average problem. Having just the *ratios* of the weights will allow you to find a weighted average. Simply use the numbers in the ratio as weights.

Weighted averages have become very important on the GMAT. Learn to handle them!

For instance, consider this problem:

> A mixture of "lean" ground beef (10% fat) and "super-lean" ground beef (4% fat) contains twice as much lean beef as super-lean beef. What is the percentage of fat in the mixture?

The ratio of lean beef to super-lean beef is 2 : 1, and so we can use 2 as the weight for the lean beef and 1 as the weight for the super-lean beef. The percentage of fat in the mixture is

$$\frac{(10\%)(2)+(4\%)(1)}{2+1} = \frac{24\%}{3} = 8\%$$

As required, this average falls between the two values and is closer to the value for the lean beef, which is more plentiful in the mixture. Notice that, unlike the percents in the grading problem, 4% and 10% are not "weights" in the weighted-average sense. Rather, these percents are the actual data points. Thus, they do not need to be expressed as decimals. You can solve the problem correctly if you change to decimals, but it is easier to solve if you leave the percentages as percentages.

Using Units to Determine Weights

In some situations, the proper choice of "weights" may be unclear. For instance, say that Joe drives 50 miles per hour for part of a trip and 65 miles per hour for the rest of the trip, and we want to find Joe's average speed for the whole trip. This is another classic weighted average problem, but it has a twist. We could potentially weight the two speeds by how many *hours* Joe spent driving at each speed, or we could weight the speeds according to how many *miles* Joe spent driving at each speed.

Here is how to decide. If you are finding a weighted average of **rates** (whose units are fractions), then the "weights" correspond to the units appearing in the ***denominator*** of the rate. Therefore, since the units of Joe's speed are miles per hour, we would weight the different speeds by the number of *hours* (not miles) Joe drives at each speed. This result makes sense, since we are concerned with how long Joe drove at different speeds and not the distance driven.

Equivalently, to find the average speed for Joe's whole trip, you can simply divide the total distance by the total time.

Be sure to understand weighted averages conceptually; do not just learn the formula.

Median: The Middle Number

Some GMAT problems feature a second type of average: the *median*, or "middle value." The median is calculated in one of two ways, depending on the number of data points in the set.

For sets containing an ***odd*** number of values, the median is the ***unique middle value*** when the data are arranged in increasing (or decreasing) order.

For sets containing an ***even*** number of values, the median is the ***average (arithmetic mean) of the two middle values*** when the data are arranged in increasing (or decreasing) order.

The median of the set {5, 17, 24, 25, 28} is the unique middle number, 24. The median of the set {3, 4, 9, 9} is the mean of the two middle values (4 and 9), or 6.5. Notice that the median of a set containing an *odd* number of values must be a value in the set. However, the median of a set containing an *even* number of values does not have to be in the set—and indeed will not be, unless the two middle values are equal.

Medians of Sets Containing Unknown Values

Unlike the arithmetic mean, the median of a set depends only on the one or two values in the middle of the ordered set. Therefore, you may be able to determine a specific value for the median of a set *even if one or more unknowns are present.*

For instance, consider the unordered set {x, 2, 5, 11, 11, 12, 33}. No matter whether x is less than 11, equal to 11, or greater than 11, the median of the resulting set will be 11. (Try substituting different values of x to see why the median does not change.)

By contrast, the median of the unordered set {x, 2, 5, 11, 12, 12, 33} depends on x. If x is 11 or less, the median is 11. If x is between 11 and 12, the median is x. Finally, if x is 12 or more, the median is 12.

Double-Barreled Average Problems

Because the median and arithmetic mean are closely related, they often appear together in problems such as this one:

> Given the set {x, x, y, y, y, y}, where $x < y$, is the median greater than the arithmetic mean?

Since the set is already in ascending order, the median must be the average of y and y, which is just y. The arithmetic mean is $\dfrac{2x+4y}{6}$. You can now pose the question "is the median greater than the arithmetic mean?" mathematically: Is $y > \dfrac{2x+4y}{6}$?

Manipulate this "question–inequality" exactly as you would a regular inequality, but remember that it is not a statement of truth by keeping a question mark on the end.

To find the median, list the numbers in the set from least to greatest, and take the middle number.

$$y > \frac{2x+4y}{6}?$$ "Is y greater than $\frac{2x+4y}{6}$?"

$6y > 2x + 4y$?   "Is 6y greater than $2x + 4y$?"

$2y > 2x$?   "Is 2y greater than $2x$?"

$y > x$?   "Is y greater than x?"

Since you know that $y > x$, your answer to the original question is "yes": the median is indeed bigger than the mean.

Alternatively, you can solve this problem with the conceptual properties of weighted averages, as discussed earlier. The mean of the set is the weighted average of four x's and two y's, which is a value between x and y. Since the median is y itself, it must be larger than the mean.

Make sure that you never confuse median and mean!

Entirely Unknown Sets

Occasionally, a problem may require you to construct and manipulate completely abstract sets. If this happens, you can use *alphabetical order* to make the set a little more concrete. For instance, if a question prompt states that "*S* is a set containing six distinct integers," then you can call those integers *A*, *B*, *C*, *D*, *E*, and *F*, in increasing order. Alternatively, you can place the variables on an abstract number line, in order to visualize their relationships.

Solve "double-barreled" average problems by writing expressions for both the median and the arithmetic mean.

Standard Deviation

The mean and median both give "average" or "representative" values for a set, but they do not tell the whole story. It is possible for two sets to have the same average but to differ widely in how spread out their values are. To describe the spread, or variation, of the data in a set, we use a different measure: the Standard Deviation.

Standard Deviation (SD) indicates how far from the average (mean) the data points typically fall. Therefore:

A small SD indicates that a set is clustered closely around the average (mean) value.

A large SD indicates that the set is spread out widely, with some points appearing far from the mean.

Consider the sets {5, 5, 5, 5}, {2, 4, 6, 8}, and {0, 0, 10, 10}. These sets all have the same mean value of 5. You can see at a glance, though, that the sets are very different, and the differences are reflected in their SDs. The first set has a SD of zero (no spread at all), the second set has a moderate SD, and the third set has a large SD.

	Set 1	Set 2	Set 3
	{5, 5, 5, 5}	{2, 4, 6, 8}	{0, 0, 10, 10}
Difference from the mean of 5 (in absolute terms)	{0, 0, 0, 0} average spread = 0 SD = 0	{3, 1, 1, 3} average spread = 2 SD = moderate (technically, SD = $\sqrt{5} \cong 2.24$)	{5, 5, 5, 5} average spread = 5 SD = large (technically, SD = 5)

You might be asking where the $\sqrt{5}$ comes from in the technical definition of SD for the second set. The good news is that you do not need to know—**it is very unlikely that a GMAT problem will ask you to calculate an exact SD**. (If you're really curious, see p. 115 of the 11th edition of the Official Guide.) If you just pay attention to what the *average spread* is doing, you'll be able to answer all GMAT standard deviation problems, which involve either (a) *changes* in the SD when a set is transformed or (b) *comparisons* of the SDs of two or more sets. Just remember that the more spread out the numbers, the larger the SD.

If you see a problem focusing on changes in the SD, ask yourself whether the changes move the data closer to the mean, farther from the mean, or neither. If you see a problem requiring comparisons, ask yourself which set is more spread out from its mean.

It is more important to understand what the standard deviation means than to learn how to calculate it.

Following are some sample problems to help illustrate standard deviation properties:

    (a) Which set has the greater standard deviation: {1, 2, 3, 4, 5} or {440, 442, 443, 444, 445}?

    (b) If each data point in a set is increased by 7, does the set's standard deviation increase, decrease, or remain constant?

    (c) If each data point in a set is increased by a factor of 7, does the set's standard deviation increase, decrease, or remain constant?

(a) The second set has the greater SD. One way to understand this is to observe that the gaps between its numbers are, on average, slightly bigger than the gaps in the first set (because the first 2 numbers are 2 units apart). Another way to resolve the issue is to observe that the set {441, 442, 443, 444, 445} would have the same standard deviation as {1, 2, 3, 4, 5}. Replacing 441 with 440, which is farther from the mean, will increase the SD.

In any case, only the *spread* matters. The numbers in the second set are much more "consistent" in some sense—they are all within about 1% of each other, while the largest numbers in the first set are several times the smallest ones. However, this "percent variation" idea is irrelevant to the SD.

(b) The SD will not change. "Increased by 7" means that the number 7 is *added* to each data point in the set. This transformation will not affect any of the gaps between the data points, and thus it will not affect how far the data points are from the mean. If the set were plotted on a number line, this transformation would merely slide the points 7 units to the right, taking all the gaps, and the mean, along with them.

(c) The SD will increase. "Increased by a *factor* of 7" means that each data point is multiplied by 7. This transformation will make all the gaps between points 7 times as big as they originally were. Thus, each point will fall 7 times as far from the mean. The SD will increase by a factor of 7.

> To see how a standard deviation changes, think about what happens to the average spread of the numbers around the mean.

Two Time-Saving Shortcuts for Averages (Advanced)

While virtually all problems about averages can be solved with some version of the basic formula, some of them can be attacked more efficiently with specialized shortcuts. Note that neither of the following shortcuts is mission-critical. Since they are both derived from the average law, they do not contain any new mathematics. However, if you master these methods, you can save valuable time on certain problems on the GMAT.

Changes to the Mean

Some arithmetic-mean problems focus exclusively on *changes* to the mean, rather than on computation of the mean itself. Especially in advanced data-sufficiency problems, you may be presented with enough information to compute how much an average will change when a new data point is inserted—despite *not* having enough information to compute the actual value of the mean.

You can compute the effect of a new data point on the existing average of a set with the following formula, which can be derived from the average law:

$$\text{Change in mean} = \frac{\text{New term} - \text{Old mean}}{\text{New number of terms}}$$

This method, although awkward when written as a formula, is easy to use in practice. For instance, if a set currently has 9 terms and a mean value of 56, and you add a tenth term of 71, then the mean will increase by $(71 - 56)/10 = 1.5$.

You can interpret this formula conceptually as taking the "excess" or "deficit" in the new term relative to the mean and redistributing that excess (or deficit) evenly to all of the terms in the set, including that new term. For instance, in the example above, the new term (71) exceeds the average by $71 - 56 = 15$. When you add the new term to the set, those 15 "extra points" are distributed evenly among all ten data points, increasing each by 1.5.

You can use this new formula on the problem about Sam's commissions from the beginning of the chapter: *Change in mean* is $100, and *New term − Old mean* is $1200. The formula yields at once the fact that Sam has made 12 sales (*New number of terms*). Be sure to distinguish old and new quantities: note that the numerator of this formula subtracts the *old* mean from the *new* term.

Another way to approach this type of problem is to pretend that all the old values equal the mean. For instance, if a set currently has 9 terms and a mean value of 56, you can simply pretend that every one of the terms equals 56. Of course, this assumption changes the standard deviation, but in these problems, you can ignore the standard deviation. This assumption will often make it very straightforward to determine the change in the mean using the standard average formula.

A change to a mean can be computed without knowing all the terms in the set.

Using Residuals

Some problems ask you to design a set with a predetermined mean, instead of computing the mean of a known set. Again, you can solve these problems with the basic formula, but you can sometimes save lots of time by using *residuals*. Residuals are the *differences* between a set's data points and its average. These differences are positive for points above the mean and negative for points below the mean. In other words,

$$Residual = Data\ point - Mean$$

You can think of residuals as "overs and unders" relative to the mean. The "overs" are positive differences from the mean, and the "unders" are negative differences from the mean. For instance, if the class average on a test is 85 points, then a score of 91 has a residual of +6 (6 over the mean of 85). Likewise, a score of 75 has a residual of −10 (10 under the mean of 85). Note that we keep track of signs for residuals. (In contrast, when we deal with standard deviation, we only care about *absolute* differences from the mean.)

To simplify your calculations, use residuals, which are "overs and unders" relative to the mean.

You only need to know one thing about residuals: **for any set, the residuals sum to zero.** Alternatively, **the positive residuals ("overs") and negative residuals ("unders") for any set will cancel out.**

Consider the following problem:

> If the mean of the set {97, 100, 85, 90, 94, 80, 92, x} is 91, what is the value of x?

You could certainly solve this problem with the traditional formula for averages, but you would waste a lot of time on arithmetic. Instead, just use the given mean of 91 to compute the residuals for all the terms except x: +6, +9, −6, −1, +3, −11, +1. These residuals sum to +1. Therefore, x must leave a residual of −1, since all the residuals sum to zero. As a result, x is one less than the mean, or 90.

Problem Set

1. The average of 11 numbers is 10. When one number is eliminated, the average of the remaining numbers is 9.3. What is the eliminated number?

2. The average of 9, 11, and 16 is equal to the average of 21, 4.6, and what number?

3. Given the set of numbers {4, 5, 5, 6, 7, 8, 21}, how much higher is the mean than the median?

4. The sum of 8 numbers is 168. If one of the numbers is 28, what is the average of the other 7 numbers?

5. What is the average of the set of odd numbers {5, 7, 9, . . . 303, 305}?

6. If the average of the set {5, 6, 6, 8, 9, x, y} is 6, then what is the value of $x + y$?

7. There is a set of 160 numbers, beginning at 6, with each subsequent term increasing by an increment of 3. What is the average of this set of numbers?

8. A charitable association sold an average of 66 raffle tickets per member. Among the female members, the average was 70 raffle tickets. The male to female ratio of the association is 1 : 2. What was the average number of raffle tickets sold by the male members of the association?

9. On 4 sales, Matt received commissions of $300, $40, $x, and $140. Without the $x, his average commission would be $50 lower. What is x?

10. The class mean score on a test was 60, and the standard deviation was 15. If Elena's score was within 2 standard deviations of the mean, what is the lowest score she could have received?

11. Matt gets a $1,000 commission on a big sale. This commission alone raises his average commission by $150. If Matt's new average commission is $400, how many sales has Matt made?

12. Matt starts a new job, with a goal of doubling his old average commission of $400. He takes a 10% commission, making commissions of $100, $200, $250, $700, and $1,000 on his first 5 sales. If Matt made two sales on the last day of the week, how much would Matt have had to sell in order to meet his goal?

13.   There is a set of numbers in ascending order: $\{y - x, y, y, y, y, x, x, x, x + y\}$. If the mean is 9, and the median is 7, what is x?

14.   Grace's average bowling score over the past 6 games is 150. If she wants to raise her average score by 10%, and she has two games left in the season, what must her average score on the last two games be?

15.   If the average of x and y is 50, and the average of y and z is 80, what is the value of $z - x$?

16.   On a particular exam, the boys in a history class averaged 86 points and the girls in the class averaged 80 points. If the overall class average was 82 points, what was the ratio of boys to girls in the class?

1. 17: If the average of 11 numbers is 10, their sum is $11 \times 10 = 110$. After one number is eliminated, the average is 9.3, so the sum of the 10 remaining numbers is $10 \times 9.3 = 93$. The number eliminated is the difference between these sums: $110 - 93 = 17$.

2. 10.4: $\dfrac{9+11+16}{3} = \dfrac{21+4.6+x}{3}$ $\qquad$ $9 + 11 + 16 = 21 + 4.6 + x$ $\qquad$ $x = 10.4$

3. 2: The mean of the set is the sum of the numbers divided by the number of terms: $56 \div 7 = 8$. The median is the middle number: 6. 8 is 2 greater than 6.

4. 20: The sum of the other 7 numbers is 140 ($168 - 28$). So, the average of the numbers is $140/7 = 20$.

5. 155: The average of an evenly spaced set is just the middle number, or the average of the first and last terms:

$$\frac{5+305}{2} = 155$$

6. 8: If the average of 7 terms is 6, then the sum of the terms is 7×6, or 42. The listed terms have a sum of 34. Therefore, the remaining terms, x and y, must have a sum of $42 - 34$, or 8.

7. 244.5: The average of an evenly spaced set is just the middle number, or the average of the first and last terms. The first term in this sequence is 6. The 160th term is $6 + (159 \times 3)$, or 483.

$$\frac{6+483}{2} = 244.5$$

8. 58: There are x men and $2x$ women in the charity group. All in all, $3x$ people sold $3x \times 66$ raffle tickets, or $198x$ tickets. The $2x$ women in the group sold $2x \times 70$ raffle tickets, or $140x$ tickets. Therefore, the men sold $198x - 140x$ tickets, or $58x$ tickets. Since there are x men in the group, the average number of tickets sold by the male members of the group is $58x \div x$, or 58 tickets.

If you pick $x = 1$ as a Smart Number, then you can make this math very quick and intuitive. 1 man and 2 women sell $(3)(66) = 198$ tickets. The 2 women sold $(2)(70) = 140$ tickets. Thus the man sold 58 tickets.

Alternatively, you can write the number of men and of women as separate unknowns, m and f:

$$\frac{f(70)+mx}{m+f} = 66 \qquad\qquad \frac{m}{f} = \frac{1}{2}$$

Cross-multiply the second equation to yield the relationship $f = 2m$. Then, substitute this expression for f in the first equation:

$$\frac{2m(70)+mx}{3m} = 66$$

$$\frac{140+x}{3} = 66$$

$$140 + x = 198$$

$$x = 58$$

*Manhattan*GMAT*Prep

9. **$360:** Without x, Matt's average sale is $(300 + 40 + 140) \div 3$, or $160. With x, Matt's average is $50 more, or $210. Therefore, the sum of $(300 + 40 + 140 + x) = 4(210) = 840$, and $x = \$360$.

10. **30:** Elena's score was within 2 standard deviations of the mean. Since the standard deviation is 15, her score is no more than 30 points from the mean. The lowest possible score she could have received, then, is $60 - 30$, or 30.

11. **5:** Before the $1,000 commission, Matt's average commission was $250; we can express this algebraically with the equation $S = 250n$.

After the sale, the sum of Matt's sales increased by $1,000, the number of sales made increased by 1, and his average commission was $400. We can express this algebraically with the equation:

$$S + 1,000 = 400(n + 1)$$

$$250n + 1,000 = 400(n + 1)$$
$$250n + 1,000 = 400n + 400$$
$$150n = 600$$
$$n = 4$$

Before the big sale, Matt had made 4 sales. Including the big sale, Matt has made 5 sales.

Alternatively, you can solve this problem using the "Change to the Mean" formula.

12. **$33,500:** On the first five sales, Matt earns a total of $2,250. In order for the average commission of 7 sales to be $800, the sum of those sales must be $7 \times \$800$, or $5,600.

$$A = \frac{S}{n} \quad \rightarrow \quad \frac{2250 + x}{7} = 800 \quad \rightarrow \quad 2250 + x = 5600$$

Therefore, Matt must earn an additional $5,600 − $2,250, or $3,350, in commissions. Matt's commission is 10%, so we can set up a proportion to calculate the total sales he needs to earn a commission of $3,350:

$$\frac{10}{100} = \frac{3350}{x}$$

$$x = \$33,500$$

13. **13:** The median number is the number in the middle of the set, or y. Therefore, $y = 7$. If the mean is 9, we can substitute numbers into the average formula as follows:

$$\frac{7 - x + 4(7) + 3x + x + 7}{9} = 9$$

$$3x + 42 = 81$$
$$3x = 39$$
$$x = 13$$

14. **210:** Grace wants to raise her average score by 10%. Since 10% of 150 is 15, her target average is 165. Grace's total score is 150×6, or 900. If, in 8 games, she wants to have an average score of 165, then she will need a total score of 165×8, or 1,320. This is a difference of $1,320 - 900$, or 420. Her average score in the next two games must be: $420 \div 2 = 210$.

15. **60:** The sum of two numbers is twice their average. Therefore,

$$x + y = 100 \qquad\qquad y + z = 160$$
$$x = 100 - y \qquad\qquad z = 160 - y$$

Substitute these expressions for z and x:

$$z - x = (160 - y) - (100 - y) = 160 - y - 100 + y = 160 - 100 = 60$$

Alternatively, pick Smart Numbers for x and y. Let $x = 50$ and $y = 50$ (this is an easy way to make their average equal 50). Since the average of y and z must be 80, we have $z = 110$. Therefore, $z - x = 110 - 50 = 60$.

16. $\dfrac{1}{2}$ **:** This is a weighted averages problem. Let b stand for the number of boys, and let g stand for the number of girls. If the average score for all the boys is 86, then the sum of all the boys' scores is $86b$. Likewise, the sum of all the girls' scores is $80g$. So the sum of all the scores is $86b + 80g$.

Since the average of all the scores is 82, and the overall number of scores is $b + g$, we can set up an equation using the relationship Sum = Average × Number of terms.

$$86b + 80g = 82(b + g)$$
$$86b + 80g = 82b + 82g$$
$$4b = 2g$$
$$2b = g$$

The question asks for the ratio of boys to girls, or $\dfrac{b}{g}$:

$$2b = g$$
$$\frac{b}{g} = \frac{1}{2}$$

Alternatively, you could have plugged directly into the formula for a weighted average, using b and g as the weights:

$$\frac{86b + 80g}{b + g} = 82$$

This equation becomes $86b + 80g = 82(b + g)$, and from this point on, the algebra is the same as above.

Chapter 7
of
WORD TRANSLATIONS

OVERLAPPING SETS

In This Chapter . . .

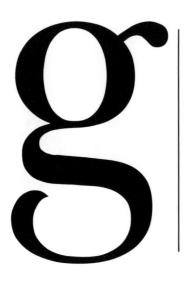

- The Double-Set Matrix
- Overlapping Sets and Percents
- Overlapping Sets and Algebraic Representation
- 3-Set Problems: Venn Diagrams

OVERLAPPING SETS

Translation problems which involve 2 or more given sets of data that partially intersect with each other are termed Overlapping Sets. For example:

> 30 people are in a room. 20 of them play golf. 15 of them play golf and tennis. If everyone plays at least one of the two sports, how many of the people play tennis only?

This problem involves two sets: (1) people who play golf and (2) people who play tennis. The two sets overlap because some of the people who play golf also play tennis. Thus, these 2 sets can actually be divided into 4 categories:

(1)   People who only play golf   (3)   People who play golf and tennis
(2)   People who only play tennis   (4)   People who play neither sport

Solving double-set GMAT problems, such as the example above, involves finding values for these four categories.

Use a double-set matrix to solve problems that involve overlapping sets.

The Double-Set Matrix

For GMAT problems involving only *two* categorizations or decisions, the most efficient tool is the *Double-Set Matrix*: a table whose rows correspond to the options for one decision, and whose columns correspond to the options for the other decision. The last row and the last column contain totals, so the bottom right corner contains the total number of everything or everyone in the problem.

Even if you are accustomed to using Venn diagrams for these problems, you should switch to the double-set matrix for problems with only two sets of options. The double-set matrix conveniently displays *all* possible combinations of options, including totals, whereas the Venn diagram only displays a few of them easily.

> Of 30 integers, 15 are in set A, 22 are in set B, and 8 are in both set A and B. How many of the integers are in NEITHER set A nor set B?

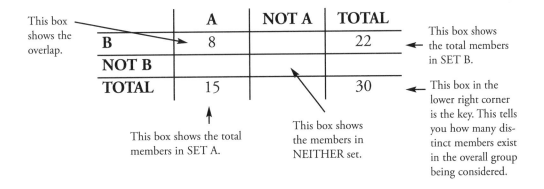

This box shows the overlap. → | | **A** | **NOT A** | **TOTAL** |
|-------|-------|-----------|-----------|
| **B** | 8 | | 22 | ← This box shows the total members in SET B.
| **NOT B** | | | |
| **TOTAL** | 15 | | 30 | ← This box in the lower right corner is the key. This tells you how many distinct members exist in the overall group being considered.

This box shows the total members in SET A.

This box shows the members in NEITHER set.

OVERLAPPING SETS STRATEGY

Once the information given in the problem has been filled in, complete the chart, using the totals to guide you. (Each row and each column sum to a total value.)

	A	NOT A	TOTAL
B	8	**14**	22
NOT B	7	**1**	**8**
TOTAL	15	**15**	30

The question asks for the number of integers in neither set. We look at the chart and find the number of integers that are NOT A and NOT B; we find that the answer is 1.

Make sure that the column labels represent <u>opposite</u> situations. Do the same for the row labels.

When you construct a double-set matrix, be careful! As mentioned above, the rows should correspond to the *mutually exclusive options* for one decision. Likewise, the columns should correspond to the mutually exclusive options for the other. For instance, if a problem deals with students getting either right or wrong answers on problems 1 and 2, the columns should **not** be "problem 1" and "problem 2," and the rows should **not** be "right" and "wrong." Instead, the columns should list options for *one* decision—problem 1 correct, problem 1 incorrect, total—and the rows should list options for the other decision—problem 2 correct, problem 2 incorrect, total.

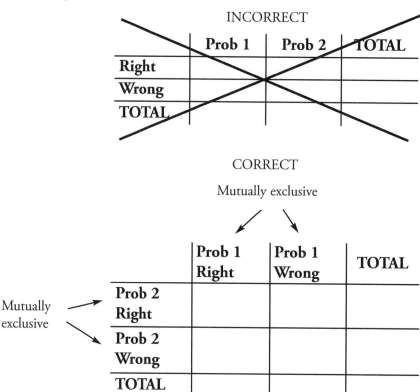

Overlapping Sets and Percents

Many overlapping-sets problems involve *percents* or *fractions*. The double-set matrix is still effective on these problems, especially if you pick a "Smart Number" for the grand total. For problems involving percents, pick a total of 100. For problems involving fractions, pick a common denominator for the total. For example, pick 15 or 30 if the problem mentions categories that are 1/3 and 2/5 of the total.

> 70% of the guests at Company X's annual holiday party are employees of Company X. 10% of the guests are women who are not employees of Company X. If half the guests at the party are men, what percent of the guests are female employees of Company X?

First, fill in 100 for the total number of guests at the party. Then, fill in the other information given in the problem: 70% of the guests are employees, and 10% are women who are not employees. We also know that half the guests are men. (Therefore, we also know that half the guests are women.)

The "smart" number for percents is 100.

	Men	Women	TOTAL
Employee			70
Not Emp.		10	
TOTAL	50	50	100

Next, use subtraction to fill in the rest of the information in the matrix:
$100 - 70 = 30$ guests who are not employees
$30 - 10 = 20$ men who are not employees
$50 - 10 = 40$ female employees

	Men	Women	TOTAL
Employee	30	40	70
Not Emp.	20	10	30
TOTAL	50	50	100

40% of the guests at the party are female employees of Company X. Note that the problem does not require us to complete the matrix with the number of male employees, since we have already answered the question asked in the problem. However, completing the matrix is an excellent way to check your computation. The last box you fill in must work both vertically and horizontally.

As in other problems involving Smart Numbers, you can only assign a number to the total if it is **undetermined** to start with. If the problem contains only fractions and/or percents, but no actual *numbers* of items or people, then go ahead and pick a total of 100 (for percent problems) or a common denominator (for fraction problems). But if actual quantities appear anywhere in the problem, then all the totals are already determined. In that case, you cannot assign numbers, but must solve for them instead.

Overlapping Sets and Algebraic Representation

When solving overlapping sets problems, you must pay close attention to the wording of the problem. For example, consider the problem below:

> Santa estimates that 10% of the children in the world have been good this year but do not celebrate Christmas, and that 50% of the children who celebrate Christmas have been good this year. If 40% of the children in the world have been good, what percentage of children in the world are not good and do not celebrate Christmas?

Read the problem very carefully to determine whether you need to use algebra to represent unknowns.

It is tempting to fill in the number 50 to represent the percent of good children who celebrate Christmas. However, this approach is incorrect.

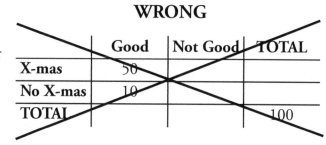

WRONG

	Good	Not Good	TOTAL
X-mas	50		
No X-mas	10		
TOTAL			100

Notice that we are told that 50% of the children *who celebrate Christmas* have been good. This is different from being told that 50% of the children in the world have been good. In this problem,

CORRECT

	Good	Not Good	TOTAL
X-mas	$0.5x$		x
No X-mas	10		
TOTAL	40		100

this information we have is a fraction of an unknown number. We do not yet know how many children celebrate Christmas. Therefore, we cannot yet write a number for the good children who celebrate Christmas. Instead, we represent the unknown total number of children who celebrate Christmas with the variable x. Thus, we can represent the number of good children who celebrate Christmas with the expression $0.5x$.

From the relationships in the table, we can set up an equation to solve for x.

$$0.5x + 10 = 40$$
$$x = 60$$

With this information, we can fill in the rest of the table.

	Good	Not Good	TOTAL
X-mas	$0.5x = 30$	30	$x = 60$
No X-mas	10	30	40
TOTAL	40	60	100

30% of the children are not good and do not celebrate Christmas.

3-Set Problems: Venn Diagrams

Problems that involve 3 overlapping sets can be solved by using a Venn Diagram.

> Workers are grouped by their areas of expertise and are placed on at least one team. 20 workers are on the Marketing team, 30 are on the Sales team, and 40 are on the Vision team. 5 workers are on both the Marketing and Sales teams, 6 workers are on both the Sales and Vision teams, 9 workers are on both the Marketing and Vision teams, and 4 workers are on all three teams. How many workers are there in total?

In order to solve this problem, use a Venn Diagram. A Venn Diagram should be used ONLY for problems that involve three sets. Stick to the double-set matrix for two-set problems.

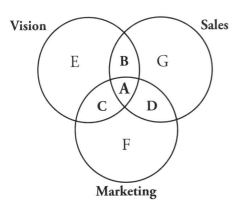

Begin your Venn Diagram by drawing three overlapping circles and labeling each one.

Notice that there are 7 different sections in a Venn Diagram. There is one innermost section (**A**) where all 3 circles overlap. This contains individuals who are on all 3 teams. There are three sections (**B, C, and D**) where 2 circles overlap. These contain individuals who are on 2 teams. There are three non-overlapping sections (**E, F, and G**) that contain individuals who are on only 1 team.

When you use a Venn Diagram, work from the INSIDE OUT.

Venn Diagrams are easy to work with, if you remember one simple rule: **Work from the Inside Out.**

That is, it is easiest to begin by filling in a number in the innermost section (**A**). Then, fill in numbers in the middle sections (**B, C, and D**). Fill in the outermost sections (**E, F, and G**) last.

First: Workers on all 3 teams: Fill in the innermost circle. This is given in the problem as 4.

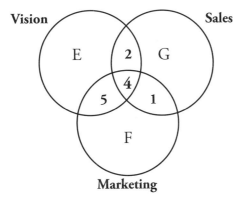

Second: <u>Workers on 2 teams:</u> Here we must remember to subtract those workers who are on all 3 teams. For example, the problem says that there are 5 workers on the Marketing and Sales teams. However, this includes the 4 workers who are on all three teams. Therefore, in order to determine the number of workers who are on the Marketing and Sales teams exclusively, we must subtract the 4 workers who are on all three teams. We are left with 5 – 4 = 1. The number of workers on the Marketing and Vision teams exclusively is 9 – 4 = 5. The number of workers on the Sales and Vision teams exclusively is 6 – 4 = 2.

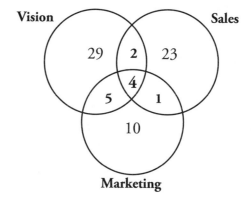

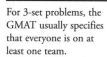
For 3-set problems, the GMAT usually specifies that everyone is on at least one team.

Third: <u>Workers on 1 team only:</u> Here we must remember to subtract those workers who are on 2 teams and those workers who are on 3 teams. For example, the problem says that there are 20 workers on the Marketing team. But this includes the 1 worker who is on the Marketing and Sales teams, the 5 workers who are on the Marketing and Vision teams, and the 4 workers who are on all three teams. We must subtract all of these workers to find that there are 20 – 1 – 5 – 4 = 10 people who are on the Marketing team exclusively. There are 30 – 1 – 2 – 4 = 23 people on the Sales team exclusively. There are 40 – 2 – 5 – 4 = 29 people on the Vision team exclusively.

In order to determine the total, just add all 7 numbers together = 74 total workers.

Problem Set

1. X and Y are sets of integers. X | Y denotes the set of integers that belong to set X or set Y, but not both. If X consists of 10 integers, Y consists of 18 integers, and 5 of the integers are in both X and Y, then X | Y consists of how many integers?

2. All of the members of Gym 1 live in Building A or Building B. There are 350 members of Gym 1. 200 people live in Building A across the street. 400 people live in Building B. 100 people from Building A are members of Gym 1. How many people live in Building B that do not belong to Gym 1?

3. Of 28 people in a park, 12 are children and the rest are adults. 8 people have to leave at 3pm; the rest do not. If after 3pm, there are 6 children still in the park, how many adults are still in the park?

4. Of 30 snakes at the reptile house, 10 have stripes, 21 are poisonous, and 5 have no stripes and are not poisonous. How many of the snakes have stripes AND are poisonous?

5. There are 30 stocks. 8 are volatile; the rest are blue-chip. 14 are tech; the rest are non-tech. If there are 3 volatile tech stocks, how many blue-chip non-tech stocks are there?

6. Students are in clubs as follows: Science–20, Drama–30, and Band–12. No student is in all three clubs, but 8 are in both Science and Drama, 6 are in both Science and Band, and 4 are in Drama and Band. How many different students are in at least one of the three clubs?

7. 40% of all high school students hate roller coasters; the rest love them. 20% of those students who love roller coasters own chinchillas. What percentage of students love roller coasters but do not own a chinchilla?

8. There are 26 students who have read a total of 56 books among them. The only books they have read, though, are Aye, Bee, Cod, and Dee. If 10 students have only read Aye, and 8 students have read only Cod and Dee, what is the smallest number of books any of the remaining students could have read?

9. Scout candies come in red, white, or blue. They can also be hard or soft. There are 50 candies: 20 red, 20 white, and 10 blue. There are 25 hard and 25 soft. If there are 5 soft blue candies and 12 soft red candies, how many hard white candies are there?

10.   Of 60 children, 30 are happy, 10 are sad, and 20 are neither happy nor sad. There are 20 boys and 40 girls. If there are 6 happy boys and 4 sad girls, how many boys are neither happy nor sad?

11.   10% of all aliens are capable of intelligent thought and have more than 3 arms, and 75% of aliens with 3 arms or less are capable of intelligent thought. If 40% of all aliens are capable of intelligent thought, what percent of aliens have more than 3 arms?

12.   There are three country clubs in town: Abacus, Bradley, and Claymore. Abacus has 300 members, Bradley 400, and Claymore has 450. 30 people belong to both Abacus and Bradley, 40 to both Abacus and Claymore, and 50 to both Bradley and Claymore. 20 people are members of all three clubs. How many people belong to at least 1 country club in town?

13.   There are 58 vehicles in a parking lot. 24 are trucks, 30 are cars, and the rest are some other vehicle. 20 of the vehicles are red, 16 are blue, and the rest are some other color. If there are 12 red trucks in the parking lot, 5 blue trucks, and 4 red cars, what is the largest possible number of blue cars in the parking lot?

14.   The 38 movies in the video store fall into the following three categories: 10 action, 20 drama, and 18 comedy. However, some movies are classified under more than one category: 5 are both action and drama, 3 are both action and comedy, and 4 are both drama and comedy. How many action–drama–comedies are there?

15.   There are 6 stores in town that had a total of 20 visitors on a particular day. However, only 10 people went shopping that day; some people visited more than one store. If 6 people visited exactly two stores each, and everyone visited at least one store, what is the largest number of stores anyone could have visited?

1. **18:** Use a Double-Set Matrix to solve this problem. First, fill in the numbers given in the problem: There are 10 integers in set X and 18 integers in set Y. There are 5 integers that are in both sets. Then, use subtraction to figure out that there are 5 integers that are in set X and not in set Y, and 13 integers that are in set Y and not in set X. This is all the information you need to solve this problem: X | Y = 5 + 13 = 18.

	Set X	NOT Set X	TOTAL
Set Y	5	**13**	18
NOT Set Y	5		
TOTAL	10		

2. **150:** Use a Double-Set Matrix to solve this problem. First, fill in the numbers given in the problem: 350 people who belong to the gym, 200 people who live in Building A, 400 people who live in Building B, and 100 gym members from Building A. Then, use subtraction to figure out that there are 250 people from Building B who belong to the gym and 150 people from Building B who do not belong to the gym.

	Building A	Building B	TOTAL
Gym	100	**250**	350
NOT Gym		**150**	
TOTAL	200	400	

3. **14:** Use a Double-Set Matrix to solve this problem. First, fill in the numbers given in the problem: 28 total people in the park, 12 children and the rest (16) adults; 8 leave at 3 pm and the rest (20) stay. Then, we are told that there are 6 children left in the park after 3pm. Since we know there are a total of 20 people in the park after 3pm, the remaining 14 people must be adults.

	Children	Adults	TOTAL
Leave at 3			8
Stay	6	**14**	**20**
TOTAL	12	16	28

4. **6:** Use a Double-Set Matrix to solve this problem. First, fill in the numbers given in the problem: 30 snakes, 10 with stripes (and therefore 20 without), 21 that are poisonous (and therefore 9 that are not), and 5 that are neither striped nor poisonous. Use subtraction to fill in the rest of the chart. 6 snakes have stripes and are poisonous.

	Stripes	No Stripes	TOTAL
Poisonous	**6**		21
NOT Poison	**4**	5	**9**
TOTAL	10	**20**	30

5. **11:** Use a Double-Set Matrix to solve this problem. First, fill in the numbers given in the problem. There are 30 stocks. 8 are volatile; the rest are blue-chip. 14 are tech; the rest are non-tech. We also know that there are 3 volatile tech stocks. Therefore, by subtraction, there are 5 volatile non-tech stocks, and there are 11 blue-chip non-tech stocks.

	Volatile	Blue-Chip	TOTAL
Tech	3		14
Non-Tech	**5**	**11**	**16**
TOTAL	8	22	30

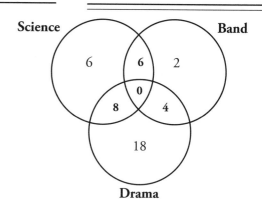

6. **44:** There are three overlapping sets here. Therefore, use a Venn diagram to solve the problem. First, fill in the numbers given in the problem, working from the inside out: no students in all three clubs, 8 in Science and Drama, 6 in Science and Band, and 4 in Drama and Band. Then, use the totals for each club to determine how many students are in only one club. For example, we know that there are 30 students in the Drama club. So far, we have placed 12 students in the circle that represents the Drama club (8 who are in Science and Drama, and 4 who are in Band and Drama). $30 - 12 = 18$, the number of students who are in only the Drama Club. Use this process to determine the number of students in just the Science and Band clubs as well. To find the number of students in at least one of the clubs, sum all the numbers in the diagram: $6 + 18 + 2 + 6 + 8 + 4 = 44$.

7. **48:** Since all the numbers in this problem are given in percentages, assign a grand total of 100 students. We know that 40% of all high school students hate roller coasters, so we fill in 40 for this total and 60 for the number of students who love roller coasters. We also know that 20% **of those students who love roller coasters** own

	Love R.C.	Do not	TOTAL
Chinchilla	12		
No Chinch.	48		
TOTAL	60	40	100

chinchillas. It does not say that 20% of all students own chinchillas. Since 60% of students love roller coasters, 20% of 60% own chinchillas. Therefore, we fill in 12 for the students who both love roller coasters and own chinchillas. The other 48 roller coaster lovers do not own chinchillas.

8. **2:** According to the problem, 10 students have read only 1 book: Aye, and 8 students have read 2 books: Cod and Dee. This accounts for 18 students, who have read a total of 26 books among them. Therefore, there are 8 students left to whom we can assign books, and there are 30 books left to assign. We can assume that one of these 8 students will have read the smallest possible number if the other 7 have read the maximum number: all 4 books. If 7 students have read 4 books each, this accounts for another 28

Students	Books Read
10	10
8	16
7	28
1	2
26	56

books, leaving only 2 for the eighth student to have read. Note that it is impossible for the eighth student to have read only one book. If we assign one of the students to have read only 1 book, this leaves 29 books for 7 students. This is slightly more than 4 books per students. However, we know that there are only four books available. It is therefore impossible for one student to have read more than four books.

9. **12:** Use a Double-Set Matrix to solve this problem, with the "color" set divided into 3 categories instead of only 2. First, fill in the numbers given in the problem: 20 red, 20 white, and 10 blue, 25 hard and 25 soft. We also know there are 5 soft blue candies and 12 soft red candies. Therefore, by subtraction, there are 8 soft white candies, and there are 12 hard white candies.

	Red	White	Blue	TOTAL
Hard		12		25
Soft	12	8	5	25
TOTAL	20	20	10	50

10. **8:** Use a Double-Set Matrix to solve this problem, with the "mood" set divided into 3 categories instead of only 2. First, fill in the numbers given in the problem: of 60 children, 30 are happy, 10 are sad, and 20 are neither happy nor sad; 20 are boys and 40 are girls. We also know there are 6 happy boys and 4 sad girls. Therefore, by subtraction, there are 6 sad boys and there are 8 boys who are neither happy nor sad.

	Happy	Sad	Neither	TOTAL
Boys	6	6	8	20
Girls		4		40
TOTAL	30	10	20	60

11. **60%:** Since all the numbers in this problem are given in percentages, assign a grand total of 100 aliens. We know that 10% of all aliens are capable of intelligent thought and have more than 3 arms. We also know that 75% **of aliens with 3 arms or less** are capable of intelligent thought. It does not say that 75% of all aliens are capable of intelligent thought.

	Thought	No Thought	TOTAL
> 3 arms	10		$100 - x$
≤ 3 arms	$0.75x$		x
TOTAL	40		100

Therefore, assign the variable x to represent the percentage of aliens with three arms or less. Then, the percentage of aliens with three arms or less who are capable of intelligent thought can be represented by $0.75x$. Since we know that 40% of all aliens are capable of intelligent thought, we can write the equation $10 + 0.75x = 40$, or $0.75x = 30$. Solve for x: $x = 40$. Therefore, 40% of the aliens have three arms or less, and 60% of aliens have more than three arms.

12. **1050:** There are three overlapping sets here; therefore, use a Venn diagram to solve the problem. First, fill in the numbers given in the problem, working from the inside out. We know that 20 people are in all three clubs. If 30 people are in both A & B, then 10 are in A & B, but not C. If 40 people are in both A & C, then 20 are in A & C, but not B. If 50 people are in both B & C, then 30 are in B & C, but not A. Then, use the totals for each club to determine how many students are in only one club. For example, we know that Abacus has 300 members. So far, we have placed 50 people in the circle that represents Abacus (10 who are in A and B, 20 who are in A and C, and 20 who are in all three clubs). $300 - 50 = 250$, the number of people who are in only the Abacus club. Use this process to determine the number of students in just the Bradley and Claymore clubs as well. To find the number of people in at least one of the clubs, sum all the numbers in the diagram:
$250 + 340 + 380 + 10 + 20 + 30 + 20 = 1050$.

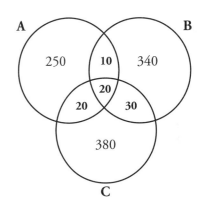

13. **11:** Use a Double-Set Matrix to solve this problem. First, fill in the numbers given in the problem: 58 vehicles are in a parking lot. 24 are trucks, 30 are cars, and the rest some other vehicle. 20 of the vehicles are red, 16 are blue, and the rest are some other color. We also know there are 12 red trucks, 5 blue trucks, and 4 red cars. The critical total in this problem is that there are 16 blue vehicles. Since 5 of them are blue trucks, and (by filling in the matrix we see that) there are 0 "other" blue vehicles, there must be 11 blue cars in the lot.

	Trucks	Cars	Other	TOTAL
Red	12	4	4	20
Blue	5		0	16
Other	7			22
TOTAL	24	30	4	58

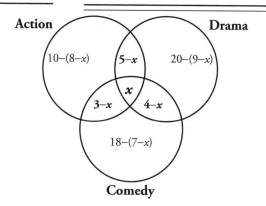

14. **2:** There are three overlapping sets here; therefore, use a Venn diagram to solve the problem. First, fill in the numbers given in the problem, working from the inside out. Assign the variable x to represent the number of action–drama–comedies. Then, create variable expressions, using the totals given in the problem, to represent the number of movies in each of the other categories. We know that there is a total of 38 movies; therefore, we can write the following equation to represent the total number of movies in the store:

$$10 - 8 + x$$
$$20 - 9 + x$$
$$18 - 7 + x$$
$$5 - x$$
$$4 - x$$
$$3 - x$$
$$+ \qquad x$$
$$\overline{36 + x = 38}$$
$$x = 2$$

If you are unsure of the algebraic solution, you can also guess a number for x and fill in the rest of the diagram until the total number of movies reaches 38.

15. **5:** If 6 people visited exactly 2 stores each, this accounts for 12 of the visitors counted in the total. This leaves 4 people to account for the remaining 8 visitors. In order to assign the maximum number of stores to any one person, assign the minimum to the first three of the remaining people: 1 store. This leaves 5 stores for the fourth person to visit.

People	Store Visits
6	12
3	3
1	5
10	20

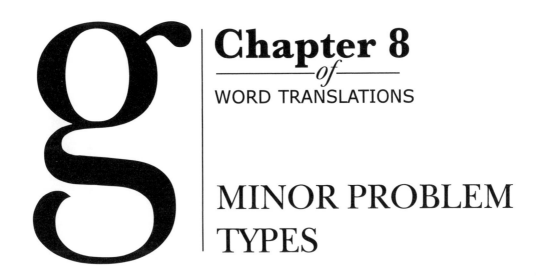

Chapter 8
of
WORD TRANSLATIONS

MINOR PROBLEM TYPES

In This Chapter . . .

- Optimization, Grouping, and Scheduling
- Computation Problems
- Graphing Problems

MINOR PROBLEM TYPES

The GMAT occasionally contains problems that fall under one of three umbrellas:

    a. *Optimization*: maximizing or minimizing a quantity by choosing optimal values of related quantities.

    b. *Grouping*: putting people or items into different groups to maximize or minimize some characteristic.

    c. *Scheduling*: planning a timeline to coordinate events according to a set of restrictions.

You should approach all three of these problem types with the same general outlook, although it is unlikely that you will see more than one of them on the same administration of the GMAT. The general approach is to focus on **extreme scenarios**.

You should mind the following three considerations when considering any grouping, scheduling, or optimization problem:

    1. Be aware of both **_explicit constraints_** (restrictions actually stated in the text) and **_hidden constraints_** (restrictions implied by the real-world aspects of a problem). For instance, in a problem requiring the separation of 40 people into 6 groups, hidden constraints require the number of people in each group to be a positive whole number.

    2. In most cases, you can maximize or minimize quantities (or optimize schedules, etc.) by **_choosing the highest or lowest values_** of the variables that you are allowed to select.

    3. Be very careful about **_rounding_**. Some problems may require you to round up, others down, and still others not at all.

Optimization

In general optimization problems, you are asked to maximize or minimize some quantity, given constraints on other quantities. These quantities are all related through some equation.

Consider the following problem:

> The guests at a football banquet consumed a total of 401 pounds of food. If no individual guest consumed more than 2.5 pounds of food, what is the minimum number of guests that could have attended the banquet?

You can visualize the underlying equation in the following table:

Pounds of food per guest	×	Guests	=	Total pounds of food
At MOST 2.5 *maximize*	×	At LEAST ??? *minimize*	=	EXACTLY 401 *constant*

Notice that finding the *minimum* value of the number of guests involves using the *maximum* pounds of food per guest, because the two quantities multiply to a constant. This sort of inversion is typical.

> Just like other Word Translation problems, these minor types require an organized approach. Keep your scrap paper neat!

Begin by considering the extreme case in which each guest eats as much food as possible, or 2.5 pounds apiece. The corresponding number of guests at the banquet works out to 401/2.5 = 160.4 people.

However, you obviously cannot have a fractional number of guests at the banquet. Thus the answer must be rounded. To determine whether to round up or down, consider the explicit constraint: the amount of food per guest is a *maximum* of 2.5 pounds per guest. Therefore, the *minimum* number of guests is 160.4 (if guests could be fractional), and we must *round up* to make the number of guests an integer: 161.

Note the careful reasoning required! Although the phrase "*minimum* number of guests" may tempt you to round down, you will get an incorrect answer if you do so. In general, as you solve this sort of problem, put the extreme case into the underlying equation, and solve. Then round appropriately.

Optimization problems require you to think about the extreme scenario—and to round in the right direction.

Grouping

In grouping problems, you make complete groups of items, drawing these items out of a larger pool. The goal is to maximize or minimize some quantity, such as the number of complete groups or the number of leftover items that do not fit into complete groups. As such, these problems are really a special case of optimization. One approach is to determine the **limiting factor** on the number of complete groups. That is, if you need different types of items for a complete group, figure out how many groups you can make with each item, ignoring the other types (as if you had unlimited quantities of those other items). Then compare your results.

> Orange Computers is breaking up its conference attendees into groups. Each group must have exactly one person from Division A, two people from Division B, and three people from Division C. There are 20 people from Division A, 30 people from Division B, and 40 people from Division C at the conference. What is the smallest number of people who will not be able to be assigned to a group?

The first step is to find out how many groups you can make with the people from each division separately, ignoring the other divisions. There are enough Division A people for 20 groups, but only enough Division B people for 15 groups (= 30 people ÷ 2 people per group). As for Division C, there are only enough people for 13 groups, since 40 people ÷ 3 people per group = 13 groups, plus one person left over. So the limiting factor is Division C: only 13 complete groups can be formed. These 13 groups will take up 13 Division A people (leaving 20 – 13 = 7 left over) and 26 Division B people (leaving 30 – 26 = 4 left over). Together with the 1 Division C person left over, 1 + 4 + 7 = 12 people will be left over in total.

For some grouping problems, you may want to think about the **most or least evenly distributed** arrangements of the items. That is, assign items to groups as evenly (or unevenly) as possible to create extreme cases.

Scheduling

Scheduling problems, which require you to determine possible schedules satisfying a variety of constraints, can usually be tackled by careful consideration of *extreme possibilities*, usually the earliest and latest possible time slots for the events to be scheduled. Consider the following problem:

> How many days after the purchase of Product X does its standard warranty expire? (1997 is not a leap year.)
> (1) When Mark purchased Product X in January 1997, the warranty did not expire until March 1997.
> (2) When Santos purchased Product X in May 1997, the warranty expired in May 1997.

Rephrase the two statements in terms of extreme possibilities:
(1) Shortest possible warranty period: Jan. 31 to Mar. 1 (29 days later)
   Longest possible warranty period: Jan. 1 to Mar. 31 (89 days later)
   Note that 1997 was not a leap year.
(2) Shortest possible warranty period: May 1 to May 2, or similar (1 day later)
   Longest possible warranty period: May 1 to May 31 (30 days later)

Even taking both statements together, there are still two possibilities—29 days and 30 days —so both statements together are still insufficient.

Note that, had the given year been a leap year, the two statements together would have become sufficient! Moral of the story: *Read the problem very, very carefully.*

Focus on the extreme possibilities to solve scheduling problems.

Computation Problems

Very occasionally, the GMAT features problems centered on computation—problems that contain no variables at all, and in principle require nothing more than "plug and chug" techniques. Sometimes, however, these problems compensate for the lack of variables with correspondingly more difficult or obscure calculations. Most of them can be tackled with the following strategy:

- Take careful *inventory* of any and all quantities presented in the problem. Be sure to pay attention to both *numbers and units*, as the interplay between the units of different quantities may give away the correct way to relate them.
- Use the same techniques and equations that have been developed for other types of problems (especially work/rate, percent, and profit problems). If the arithmetic is complicated enough, you might want to designate variables.
- Draw a diagram, table, or chart to organize information, if necessary.
- *Read the problem carefully*, as purely computation-based problems tend to be trickier than other problems!

Here is an example:

> Five identical pieces of wire are soldered together to form a longer wire, with the pieces overlapping by 4 cm at each join. If the wire thus made is exactly 1 meter long, how long is each of the identical pieces? (1 meter = 100 cm)

A diagram is helpful for this problem. Note that, without a diagram, it is easy to assume that, because there are 5 pieces, there must be 5 joins. Instead, there are only 4 joins.

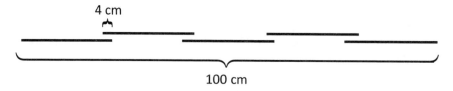

First, convert to make compatible units: 1 meter = 100 cm.

Each join includes 4 cm of *both* wires joined, but is only counted once in the total length of 100 cm. Therefore, the total length of *all* the original wires is 100 + 4(4) = 116 cm. Because there are five wires, each wire is 116/5 = 23.2 cm long. (If you prefer, you could set this problem up with a variable: $5x - 16 = 100$.)

On **data sufficiency** problems involving computation, remember that there is no need to perform computations! If you can simply establish that you have enough information to compute the answer to a problem, you have your answer ("sufficient").

Graphing Problems

Very occasionally, the GMAT will ask you to interpret a graph, table, or chart. These problems feature considerable variety, but in most cases the following tips can be helpful:
- Study the graph or table carefully *both before and after* reading the problem. When you examine the graph, pay special attention to *labels, units, and scales*.
- Look for *patterns* in the shape of graphs (or in the numbers in tables). Typical patterns include increasing values, decreasing values, and conspicuous maximum or minimum values.

Be sure to draw a picture or otherwise conceptualize any computation problem before diving into the math. There is often a trap you must avoid!

Problem Set

1. Velma has exactly one week to learn all 71 Japanese hiragana characters. If she can learn at most a dozen of them on any one day and will only have time to learn four of them on Friday, what is the least number of hiragana that Velma will have to learn on Saturday?

2. Shaggy has to learn the same 71 hiragana characters, and also has one week to do so; unlike Velma, he can learn as many per day as he wants. However, Shaggy has decided to obey the advice of a study-skills professional, who has advised him that the number of characters he learns on any one day should be within 4 of the number he learns on any other day.
    a. What is the least number of hiragana that Shaggy could have to learn on Saturday?
    b. What is the greatest number of hiragana that Shaggy could have to learn on Saturday?

3. When it is 2:01 P.M. Sunday afternoon in Nullepart, it is Monday in Eimissaan; when it is 1:00 P.M. Wednesday in Eimissaan, it is also Wednesday in Nullepart. When it is noon Friday in Nullepart, what is the possible range of times in Eimissaan?

4. Huey's Hip Pizza sells two sizes of square pizzas: a small pizza that measures 10 inches on a side and costs $10, and a large pizza that measures 15 inches on a side and costs $20. If two friends go to Huey's with $30 apiece, how many more square inches of pizza can they buy if they pool their money than if they each purchase pizza alone?

5. An eccentric casino owner decides that his casino should only use chips in $5 and $7 denominations. Which of the following amounts cannot be paid out using these chips?

    $31 $29 $26 $23 $21

6. A "Collector's Coin Set" contains a one dollar coin, a fifty-cent coin, a quarter (= 25 cents), a dime (= 10 cents), a nickel (= 5 cents), and a penny (= 1 cent). The Coin Sets are sold for the combined face price of the currency. If Colin buys as many Coin Sets as he can with the $25 he has, how much change will Colin have left over?

7. Castor trades in his old car, which traveled 16 miles per gallon of gasoline, and buys a new car that travels 20 miles per gallon. Castor's brother Pollux sells his hybrid, which traveled 50 miles per gallon, because he has built a revolutionary new car that travels 100 miles per gallon. If both brothers drive their cars 1000 miles to a family reunion, and gas costs $3.00 per gallon, which brother will have saved more money by switching cars, and by how much?

8. Municipality X taxes the annual income of individual residents at a rate of 2% of all income up to $60,000 and 4% of all income in excess of $60,000; it taxes the annual income of resident married couples at a rate of 2% of all income up to $100,000 and 4% of all income in excess of $100,000. Pete and Laura, single residents of Municipality X, each earn $80,000 per year.

    a. What percent of Pete's (or Laura's) *total* annual income is paid in municipal taxes?

    b. If Pete and Laura marry and file this year's taxes as a married couple, what percent of their *total* annual income will be paid in municipal taxes?

9. A museum offers four video programs that run continuously throughout the day, each program starting anew as soon as it is finished. The first program runs every 15 minutes, the second every 30 minutes, the third every 45 minutes, and the fourth every 40 minutes; the first show of each program starts at 10:00 A.M. and the last showing of each program ends at 4:00 P.M. If a tour group can watch the programs in any order, but needs at least ten minutes between programs to regroup, what is the least amount of time the group can take to watch all four programs?

10.

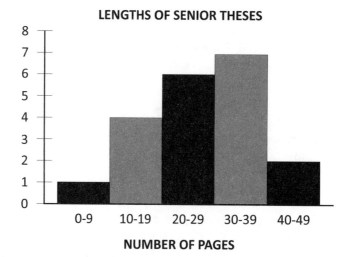

LENGTHS OF SENIOR THESES

NUMBER OF PAGES

Each senior in a college course wrote a thesis. The lengths, in pages, of those seniors' theses are summarized in the graph above.

    a. What is the *least* possible number of seniors whose theses were within six pages of the median length?

    b. What is the *greatest* possible number of seniors whose theses were within six pages of the median length?

1. **7**: To minimize the number of hiragana that Velma will have to learn on Saturday, consider the extreme case in which she learns *as many* hiragana *as possible* on the other days. She learns 4 on Friday, leaving 71 − 4 = 67 for the other six days of the week. If Velma learns the maximum of 12 hiragana on the other five days (besides Saturday), then she will have 67 − 5(12) = 7 left for Saturday.

2. a. **7**: Perhaps the most straightforward way to solve this problem is by trial and error, considering different minimum values and noting the consequences. If Shaggy learns only 7 hiragana on Saturday, then he is allowed to learn at most 11 on other days of the week, for a maximum of 7 + 6(11) = 73. That is good enough, as there are only 71 hiragana to learn (so he could learn, say, 9, 11, 11, 11, 11, 11, and 7). If Shaggy learns 6 hiragana on Saturday, though, he is only allowed to learn at most 10 on other days of the week, for a maximum of 6 + 6(10) = 66. That is not enough.

    This problem can also be solved with an inequality: $m + 6(m + 4) \geq 71$ (where m is the Saturday minimum, and $m + 4$ is the number of hiragana for each of the other days).

    b. **13**: This problem can likewise be solved by trial and error. If Shaggy learns 13 hiragana on Saturday, he must learn at least 9 on each of the other days, for a minimum of 13 + 6(9) = 67. Therefore, that will work (if he learns, say, 10, 10, 10, 10, 9, 9, 13). If Shaggy learns 14 hiragana on Saturday, though, he is committed to learning at least 10 on each of the other days, for a minimum of 14 + 6(10) = 74, but there are not that many to learn!

    This problem can also be solved with an inequality: $M + 6(M − 4) \leq 71$ (where M is the Saturday maximum, and $M − 4$ is the number of hiragana for each of the other days).

3. **Anywhere from 10 P.M. Friday to 1 A.M. Saturday**: The first statement tells you that the time in Eimissaan is at least 10 hours ahead of the time in Nullepart; given this information, the second statement tells you that the time in Eimissaan is at most 13 hours ahead of the time in Nullepart. (The second statement *by itself* could allow Nullepart time to be ahead of Eimissaan time, but that situation is already precluded by the first statement.) Therefore, the time in Eimissaan is between 10 and 13 hours ahead of the time in Nullepart.

4. **25 square inches**: First, figure the area of each pizza: the small is 100 square inches, and the large is 225 square inches.If the two friends pool their money, they can buy three large pizzas, which have a total area of 675 square inches. If they buy individually, though, then each friend will have to buy one large pizza and one small pizza, so they will only have a total of 2(100 + 225) = 650 square inches of pizza.

5. **$23**: This problem is similar to a Scheduling Problem in which you have a number of 5-hour and 7-hour tasks, and your mission is to figure out what total amount of time would be impossible to take. Either way, you have some integer number of 5's and some integer number of 7's. Which of the answer choices cannot be the sum? One efficient way to eliminate choices is first to cross off any multiples of 7 and/or 5: this eliminates E. Now, any other possible sums must have at least one 5 and one 7 in them. So you can subtract off 5's one at a time until you reach a multiple of 7. (It is easier to subtract 5's than 7's, because our number system is base-10.) Answer choice A: 31 − 5 = 26; 26 − 5 = 21, a multiple of 7; this eliminates A. (In other words, 31 = 3 × 7 + 2 × 5.) Answer choice B: 29 − 5 = 24; 24 − 5 = 19; 19 − 5 = 14, a multiple of 7; this eliminates B. Answer choice C: 26 − 5 = 21, a multiple of 7; this eliminates C. So the answer must be D, 23. We check by successively subtracting 5 and looking for multiples of 7: 23 − 5 = 18, not a multiple of 7; 18 − 5 = 13, also not a multiple of 7; 13 − 5 = 8, not a multiple of 7; and no smaller result will be a multiple of 7 either.

6. **$0.17**: The first step is to compute the value of a complete "Collector's Coin Set": $1.00 + $0.50 + $0.25 + $0.10 + $0.05 + $0.01 = $1.91. Now, you need to divide $1.91 into $25. A natural first move is to multiply by 10: for $19.10, Colin can buy 10 complete sets. Now add $1.91 successively. Colin can buy 11 sets for $21.01, 12 sets for $22.92, and 13 sets for $24.83. There are 17 cents left over.

7. **Castor saves $7.50 more**: We start out with the same known quantity (1,000 miles) for each of the brothers. Direct conversion from miles to dollars is impossible, since dollars are related only to gallons (via the price of gas); therefore, we must convert miles → gallons → dollars.

Use a rate chart similar to an *RTD* chart, but notice the difference in units (there are no time units; instead, we have miles/gallon × gallons = miles). The resulting equation is $16g = 1,000$, so $g = 62.5$ gallons.

	mi/gal		gal		mi
Castor: old car	16	×	g	=	1,000

Then, use *another RTD*-type chart, if necessary, to figure the dollar cost of those 62.5 gallons of gasoline. In this case, the equation is $(3)(62.5) = d$, so $d = 187.50.

	$/gal		gal		$
Castor: old car	3	×	62.5	=	d

Using calculations that are entirely analogous to these, Castor's new car will use 50 gallons of gasoline, costing him $150; Pollux's old hybrid would have used 20 gallons, costing him $60; and Pollux's revolutionary new car will use 10 gallons, costing him $30. Castor's net savings is $187.50 − $150 = $37.50, while Pollux's is $60 − $30 = $30.

The alternative technique of *top–bottom cancelling* with conversion factors (see p. 31) solves the problem much more quickly—in one step for each of the 4 cars:

$$\text{Castor: old car} = 1000 \text{ mi} \times \frac{1 \text{ gal}}{16 \text{ mi}} \times \frac{\$3.00}{1 \text{ gal}} = \$187.50 \text{ , and so forth.}$$

8. a. **2.5%**: Since Pete's (or Laura's) annual income is in excess of $60,000, (s)he must pay 2% of the first $60,000, or $1,200. Additionally, (s)he must pay 4% of the $20,000 excess, or $800. Therefore, Pete/Laura pays $2,000 in taxes out of $80,000 total income, or 2.5%.

b. **2.75%**: If Pete and Laura marry, their annual income will be $160,000. They will have to pay 2% of the first $100,000, or $2,000; additionally, they will have to pay 4% of the $60,000 excess, or $2,400. Therefore, they will pay $4,400 in taxes out of their $160,000 total income, or 2.75%.

9. **165 minutes (or 2 hours, 45 minutes)**: The first program plays every hour, hour:15, hour:30, and hour:45; the second plays every hour and half-hour; the third plays at 10:00, 10:45, 11:30, 12:15, and so on; the fourth plays at 10:00, 10:40, 11:20, and so on. A look at this list shows that only the fourth show is separated from any of the others by exactly 10 minutes. Thus, the fourth show should be viewed second or third (i.e., somewhere in the middle) and at one of the times that *does not* start or end on the hour, so that it is flanked by 2 waiting times of exactly 10 minutes each. The third waiting time must be at least 15 minutes, so the total time is at least the cumulative length of all four shows plus 35 minutes in waiting time, or 145 minutes. (One sample schedule that achieves this minimum: third show 10:45-11:30, fourth show 11:40-12:20, second show 12:30-1:00, first show 1:15-1:30.)

10. There are twenty seniors in the class, so the median class length is the average (arithmetic mean) of the lengths of the tenth- and eleventh-longest theses, both of which are between 20 and 29 pages (inclusive). Those two theses *must* be within six pages of the median: even if they are placed as far apart as possible (20 and 29 pages), each will be only 4.5 pages away from the median.

a. **2**: Since the tenth- and eleventh-longest papers must satisfy the criterion, place them as close together as possible (to leave room to manipulate the other lengths): say 28 pages apiece. If the other four 20- to 29-page papers are each 20 or 21 pages, and all seven 30- to 39-page papers are each 35 pages or more, then only the tenth- and eleventh-longest papers are within six pages of the mean.

b. **17**: If the tenth-longest paper is 25 pages and the eleventh-longest paper is 24 pages, then the median length is 24.5 pages, so all of the 20- to 29-page papers are within six pages of the median. If each of the four 10- to 19-page papers is 19 pages long and each of the seven 30- to 39-page papers is 30 pages long, then all eleven of those papers will also be within the desired range.

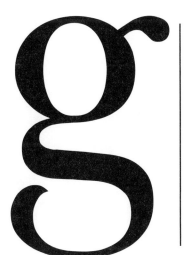

Chapter 9
of
WORD TRANSLATIONS

STRATEGIES FOR
DATA SUFFICIENCY

In This Chapter . . .

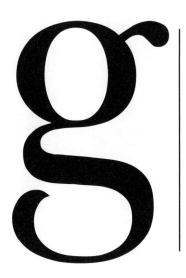

- Rephrasing: Translating Words into Algebra
- Sample Rephrasings for Challenging Problems

Rephrasing: Translating Words into Algebra

To solve word translation data sufficiency problems, you need to rephrase words into algebra. Any time you see a word problem in data sufficiency, you should immediately rephrase the information provided both in the question and in the statements. Be sure to keep track of the variables you assign to represent each unknown value. For example:

> A hot dog vendor who sells only hot dogs and soft drinks charges $3 for a hot dog. If the vendor collected $1,000 in total revenue last month, how much does he charge for a soft drink?
>
> (1) The vendor sold twice as many hot dogs as soft drinks last month.
> (2) The revenue from hot dog sales last month was 3/4 of the total monthly revenue.

(A) Statement (1) ALONE is sufficient, but statement (2) alone is not sufficient.
(B) Statement (2) ALONE is sufficient, but statement (1) alone is not sufficient.
(C) BOTH statements TOGETHER are sufficient, but NEITHER statement ALONE is sufficient.
(D) EACH statement ALONE is sufficient.
(E) Statements (1) and (2) together are NOT sufficient.

First, assign variables and rephrase the information contained in the question itself by translating the words into algebraic expressions:

> Let H = the number of hot dogs sold
> Let S = the number of soft drinks sold
> Let x = the price of soft drinks

The question can be rephrased as follows: Given that $3H + xS = 1,000$, what is x?

Statement (1) can be rephrased as **$H = 2S$**. This allows us to substitute $2S$ in for H in the original equation.

$$3H + xS = 1,000 \;\rightarrow\; 3(2S) + xS = 1,000 \;\rightarrow\; 6S + xS = 1,000$$

However, this still leaves us with 2 unknown variables. It is impossible to find the value of x without knowing the value of S. Thus, statement (1) alone is not sufficient to answer the question.

Statement (2) can be rephrased as $3H = 750$ or **$H = 250$**. We can substitute 250 for H in the original equation as follows:

$$3H + xS = 1,000 \;\rightarrow\; 3(250) + xS = 1,000 \;\rightarrow\; 750 + xS = 1,000 \;\rightarrow\; xS = 250$$

However, without knowing the value of S, this is insufficient to find the variable x. Thus, statement (2) alone is not sufficient to answer the question.

Be sure to make a note of what each variable represents.

If you combine the information given in both statements, you have two different equations with two unknown variables. Using substitution, you can solve for both S and x. Thus, the answer to this data sufficiency problem is (C): BOTH statements TOGETHER are sufficient, but NEITHER statement ALONE is sufficient.

Consider this example:

> If the price of a gallon of milk and a loaf of bread both increased by 10% from 1987 to 1990, what was the price of a loaf of bread in 1987?
>
> (1) Together, a loaf of bread and a gallon of milk cost $3.60 in 1987.
> (2) Together, a loaf of bread and a gallon of milk cost $3.96 in 1990.

First, assign variables and rephrase the information contained in the question itself.

> Let $B =$ the price of a loaf of bread in 1987
> Let $M =$ the price of a gallon of milk in 1987

The question can be rephrased as follows: What is B?

Statement (1) can be rephrased as $B + M = 3.60$. It is impossible to find the value of B without knowing the value of M. Picking extreme numbers illustrates this. The loaf of bread could have cost $3.55 and the gallon of milk $0.05. Or the reverse could have been true. Thus, statement (1) alone is NOT sufficient to answer the question.

Statement (2) can be rephrased as $1.1B + 1.1M = 3.96$. We are representing the price of a loaf of bread in 1990 as $1.1B$ because the question tells us that the price of a loaf of bread in 1990 was 10% greater than the price of a loaf of bread in 1987. The same logic holds for the price of a gallon of milk.

Notice that statement (2) can be rephrased further by dividing both sides of the equation by 1.1. This yields the following: $B + M = 3.60$. This is the same information as provided in statement (1)! As such, using the same logic as with statement (1), it is impossible to find the value of B without knowing the value of M. Thus, statement (2) alone is NOT sufficient to answer the question.

Looking at both statements together does not add any new information, since statement (2) provides the exact same information as statement (1).

The answer to this data sufficiency problem is (E): Statements (1) and (2) TOGETHER are NOT sufficient.

Remember that you can often rephrase both the question *and* the statements.

Rephrasing: Challenge Short Set

At the very end of this book, you will find lists of WORD TRANSLATIONS problems that have appeared on past official GMAT exams. These lists reference problems from *The Official Guide for GMAT Review, 11th Edition* and *The Official Guide for GMAT Quantitative Review* (the questions contained therein are the property of The Graduate Management Admission Council, which is not affiliated in any way with Manhattan GMAT).

As you work through the Data Sufficiency problems listed at the end of this book, be sure to focus on *rephrasing*. If possible, try to *rephrase* each question into its simplest form *before* looking at the two statements. In order to rephrase, focus on figuring out the specific information that is absolutely necessary to answer the question. After rephrasing the question, you should also try to *rephrase* each of the two statements, if possible. Rephrase each statement by simplifying the given information into its most basic form.

In order to help you practice rephrasing, we have taken the most difficult Data Sufficiency problems on *The Official Guide* problem list (these are the problem numbers listed in the "Challenge Short Set" on page 167) and have provided you with our own sample rephrasings for each question and statement. In order to evaluate how effectively you are using the rephrasing strategy, you can compare your rephrased questions and statements to our own rephrasings that appear below. Questions and statements that are significantly rephrased appear in **bold**.

Rephrasings from *The Official Guide For GMAT Review, 11th Edition*

The questions and statements that appear below are only our *rephrasings*. The original questions and statements can be found by referencing the problem numbers below in the Data Sufficiency section of *The Official Guide for GMAT Review, 11th Edition* (pages 278–290).

<u>Note</u>: Problem numbers preceded by "D" refer to questions in the Diagnostic Test chapter of *The Official Guide for GMAT Review, 11th Edition* (pages 24–25).

68. $A = \dfrac{j+k}{2}$

What is the value of $j + k$?

  (1) $\dfrac{j+2+k+4}{2} = 11$

  $j + k = 16$

  (2) $\dfrac{j+k+14}{3} = 10$

  $j + k = 16$

79. T = hours of additional travel time (the same for Cars X and Y)
R_x = rate of car X R_y = rate of car Y
$(T)R_x$ = distance of car X $(T)R_y$ = distance of car Y

For car X to increase its lead by 1 mile over car Y:

$(T)R_x = (T)R_y + 1$ which simplifies to $T(R_x - R_y) = 1$

What is the value of T?   **OR**   **What is the value of $R_x - R_y$?**

  (1) $R_x - R_y = 50 - 40 = 10$

  (2) In 3/60 of an hour, car X increased its lead by 1/2 mile:

  $(3/60)R_x = (3/60)R_y + 1/2$
  $R_x - R_y = 10$

82.   Let x = the probability that the chip will be red
Let y = the probability that the chip will be blue
Let z = the probability that the chip will be white

$x + y + z = 1$
$y + z = 1 - x$

What is the value of $(y + z)$?   OR   What is the value of $1 - x$?

(1) $y = \dfrac{1}{5}$

(2) $x = \dfrac{1}{3}$

94.   Let x = the number of student who DO study Spanish
       Let y = the number of students who do NOT study Spanish

	French	No French	TOTAL
Spanish	?	100	x
No Spanish		0	y
TOTAL	200	100	300

What is the value of x or y?

(1) $y = 60$
(2) $x = 240$

120.   In order to average 120 or more words per paragraph, the report would need to contain at least
       $25(120) = 3,000$ total words.

       The first 23 paragraphs of the report contain 2600 total words.

       Does the 2-paragraph preface contain fewer than 400 words?

       (1) The 2-paragraph preface contains more than 200 words.
       (2) The 2-paragraph preface contains fewer than 300 words.

155.   Let c = the capacity of the bucket

       What is the value of c?

       (1) Let x = the amount of water in the bucket
           $x = 9$

       (2) $3 + 1/2c = 4/3(1/2c)$

D27.   Let f = charge for the first minute
Let a = number of additional minutes (after the first minute)
Let r = rate for each additional minute
Let T = total cost for the call

$$T = f + a(r)$$

What is $a + 1$?   OR   What is a?

(1) $T = 6.50$

(2) $T = f + a(r)$
      $T = (r + 0.50) + a(r)$

D29.   The question itself cannot be rephrased. However, each statement can be rephrased using a double-set matrix as follows:

(1)

	Bought Business Computers	Did NOT Buy Business Computers	TOTAL
Own Store	0.85x	0.15x	x
Do NOT Own Store			
TOTAL	?		100

(2)

	Bought Business Computers	Did NOT Buy Business Computers	TOTAL
Own Store			40
Do NOT Own Store			60
TOTAL	?		100

D46.   Average salary last year for 10 employees = $42,800
Total salary paid to these 10 employees last year = $42,800(10) = $428,000

To find the average salary for these 10 employees this year:
What is the TOTAL amount paid to these 10 employees this year?

(1) Total paid to 8 employees THIS year = 1.15 × (Total paid to *these* 8 employees LAST year). We do not know the total paid to *these* 8 employees last year, so we cannot calculate this year's total.

(2) Total paid to 2 employees THIS year = Total paid to *these* 2 employees LAST year. We do not know the total paid to *these* 2 employees last year, so we cannot calculate this year's total.

Rephrasings from *The Official Guide for GMAT Quantitative Review*

The questions and statements that appear below are only our *rephrasings*. The original questions and statements can be found by referencing the problem numbers below in the Data Sufficiency section of *The Official Guide for GMAT Quantitative Review* (pages 149–157).

29.   Let c = the number of questions John answered correctly on the test

What is the value of c?

(1) Let f = the number of questions John answered correctly out of the first 30 questions
Let s = the number of questions John answered correctly out of the second 30 questions
$f = 7 + s$
$f + s = c$

(2) $c = 5/6(30) + 4/5(30)$

38.   Let x = rate of machine X
Let y = rate of machine Y

Machine X produces 100 cans in 2 hours. Therefore, $x = 50$.

What is $x + y$?   OR   What is y?

(1) $x = y$

(2) $x + y = 2x$

50.   **Can all of these variables be expressed in terms of one of the variables?**

(1) $z = 1$ AND $y = 32/x$

(2) $x = 2y$ AND $y = 4z$
$x = 2(4z) = 8z$

65.   Let c = the number of cars produced
Let t = the number of trucks produced

What is the ratio of $\dfrac{c}{t}$?

(1) $1.08c = 1.5t$

$\dfrac{c}{t} = \dfrac{1.5}{1.08}$

(2) $\dfrac{c}{t} = \dfrac{565,000}{406,800}$

71.   Does $z = 18$?

(1) $x + y + z = 18$

(2) $x = 2y$

99. 0 , x , 10

Is $z > \dfrac{x+10}{2}$?

(1) No rephrasing is possible. Test different values for z and x.

(2) $z = 5x$

107.   Testing numbers is the easiest way to solve this problem.

112. x is an integer.
       Is y an integer?

(1) $x + y + y - 2 = 3x$
    $y = x + 1$

(2) $\dfrac{x+y}{2}$ = not an integer. Test numbers to prove this information insufficient.

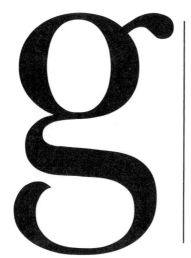

Chapter 10
of
WORD TRANSLATIONS

OFFICIAL GUIDE
PROBLEM SETS

In This Chapter . . .

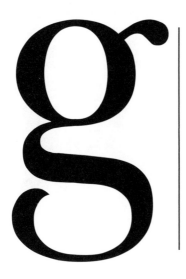

- Word Translations Problem Solving List
  from *The Official Guides*
- Word Translations Data Sufficiency List
  from *The Official Guides*

Practicing with REAL GMAT Problems

Now that you have completed your study of WORD TRANSLATIONS it is time to test your skills on problems that have actually appeared on real GMAT exams over the past several years.

The problem sets that follow are composed of questions from two books published by the Graduate Management Admission Council® (the organization that develops the official GMAT exam):

The Official Guide for GMAT Review, 11th Edition &
The Official Guide for GMAT Quantitative Review

These two books contain quantitative questions that have appeared on past official GMAT exams. (The questions contained therein are the property of The Graduate Management Admission Council, which is not affiliated in any way with Manhattan GMAT.)

Although the questions in the Official Guides have been "retired" (they will not appear on future official GMAT exams), they are great practice questions.

In order to help you practice effectively, we have categorized every problem in The Official Guides by topic and subtopic. On the following pages, you will find two categorized lists:

(1) **Problem Solving:** Lists all Problem Solving WORD TRANSLATION questions contained in *The Official Guides* and categorizes them by subtopic.

(2) **Data Sufficiency:** Lists all Data Sufficiency WORD TRANSLATION questions contained in *The Official Guides* and categorizes them by subtopic.

Note: Each book in Manhattan GMAT's 8-book strategy series contains its own *Official Guide* lists that pertain to the specific topic of that particular book. If you complete all the practice problems contained on the *Official Guide* lists in the back of each of the 8 Manhattan GMAT strategy books, you will have completed every single question published in *The Official Guides*.

Problem Solving

from *The Official Guide for GMAT Review, 11ᵗʰ Edition* (pages 20–23 & 152–186) and *The Official Guide for GMAT Quantitative Review* (pages 62–85)

<u>Note</u>: Problem numbers preceded by "D" refer to questions in the Diagnostic Test chapter of *The Official Guide for GMAT Review, 11ᵗʰ Edition* (pages 20–23). Do these problems last.

Solve each of the following problems in a notebook, making sure to demonstrate how you arrived at each answer by showing all of your work and computations. If you get stuck on a problem, look back at the WORD TRANSLATIONS strategies and content contained in this guide to assist you.

<u>CHALLENGE SHORT SET</u>
This set contains the more difficult word translation problems from each of the content areas.
> *11ᵗʰ Edition*: 64, 87, 170, 182, 193, 200, 208, 212, 217, 218, 223, 224, 239, D6, D14
> *Quantitative Review*: 23, 87, 119, 129, 130

<u>FULL PROBLEM SET</u>
Algebraic Translations
> *11ᵗʰ Edition*: 24, 47, 74, 91, 92, 140, 153, 200, 210
> *Quantitative Review*: 17, 23, 62, 76, 127, 131

Rates and Work
> *11ᵗʰ Edition*: 19, 25, 82, 87, 103, 126, 154, 185, 223
> *Quantitative Review*: 14, 20, 21, 35, 87, 90, 119, 130, 136, 140

Ratios
> *11ᵗʰ Edition*: 18, 50, 52, 61, 63, 73, 76, 97, 106, 118, 163, 168, 170, 181, 193, 196
> *Quantitative Review*: 71, 82

Combinatorics & Probability
> *11ᵗʰ Edition*: 10, 64, 121, 135, 173, 195, 217, 231, D7
> *Quantitative Review*: 80, 132, 151

Statistics
> *11ᵗʰ Edition*: 11, 54, 65, 68, 93, 101, 119, 132, 149, 182, 186, 203, 208, 212, 218, 224, D9
> *Quantitative Review*: 30, 59, 63, 70, 84, 129, 137, 148, 157, 161

Overlapping Sets
> *11ᵗʰ Edition*: 79, 169, 166, 179, 214, 239, D4, D6, D14
> *Quantitative Review*: 16

Miscellaneous (Graphs, Computation, and Non-Standard Problems)
Solve by charting, listing, drawing pictures, and employing logical reasoning.
> *11ᵗʰ Edition*: 1, 27, 32, 72, 88, 95, 116, 141
> *Quantitative Review*: 49, 50, 54, 94, 105, 110, 126, 168

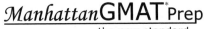

Data Sufficiency

from *The Official Guide for GMAT Review, 11th Edition* (pages 24–25 & 278–290) and *The Official Guide for GMAT Quantitative Review* (pages 149–157).

<u>Note</u>: Problem numbers preceded by "D" refer to questions in the Diagnostic Test chapter of *The Official Guide for GMAT Review, 11th Edition* (pages 24–25). Do these problems last.

Solve each of the following problems in a notebook, making sure to demonstrate how you arrived at each answer by showing all of your work. If you get stuck on a problem, look back at the WORD TRANSLATIONS strategies and content contained in this guide to assist you.

Practice REPHRASING both the questions and the statements. The majority of data sufficiency problems can be rephrased; however, if you have difficulty rephrasing a problem, try testing numbers to solve it.

CHALLENGE SHORT SET
This set contains the more difficult word translation problems from each of the content areas.
> *11th Edition*: 68, 79, 82, 94, 120, 155, D27, D29, D46
> *Quantitative Review*: 29, 38, 50, 65, 71, 99, 107, 112

FULL PROBLEM SET
Algebraic Translations
> *11th Edition*: 53, 73, 92, 98, 100, 115, 155, D27
> *Quantitative Review*: 12, 17, 26, 27, 29, 81, 93, 104

Rates and Work
> *11th Edition*: 19, 33, 63, 79, 81, 93
> *Quantitative Review*: 38, 47, 54, 69

Ratios
> *11th Edition*: 2, 95, 130, 138
> *Quantitative Review*: 11, 24, 31, 50, 65, 74

Combinatorics & Probability
> *11th Edition*: 10, 82

Statistics
> *11th Edition*: 68, 104, 114, 120, 141, D31, D32, D43, D46
> *Quantitative Review*: 34, 41, 71, 97, 99, 107, 112

Overlapping Sets
> *11th Edition*: 49, 90, 94, D29, D34, D47
> *Quantitative Review*: 10, 62

Miscellaneous (Graphs, Computation, and Non-Standard Problems)
> *11th Edition*: 13, 36, 44, 71, 87, 88, 96, 106, D45
> *Quantitative Review*: 8

To waive "Finance I" at Harvard Business School you must:

(A) Be a CFA
(B) Have prior coursework in finance
(C) Have two years of relevant work experience in the financial sector
(D) Pass a waiver exam
(E) None of the above; one cannot waive core courses at HBS

What are the requirements of an Entrepreneurial Management major at the Wharton School?

(1) Completion of 5 credit units (cu) that qualify for the major
(2) Participation in the Wharton Business Plan Competition during the 2nd year of the MBA program

(A) Statement (1) ALONE is sufficient, but statement (2) alone is not sufficient.
(B) Statement (2) ALONE is sufficient, but statement (1) alone is not sufficient.
(C) BOTH statements TOGETHER are sufficient, but NEITHER statement ALONE is sufficient.
(D) EACH statement ALONE is sufficient.
(E) Statements (1) and (2) TOGETHER are NOT sufficient.

Once You Ace the GMAT, Get Ready to Ace Your Applications!

To make an informed decision in applying to a school—and to craft an effective application that demonstrates an appreciation of a program's unique merits—**it's crucial that you do your homework**. Clear Admit School Guides cut through the gloss of marketing materials to give you the hard facts about a program, and then put these school-specific details in context so you can see how programs compare. In the guides, you'll find detailed, comparative information on vital topics such as:

- The core curriculum and first-year experience
- Leading professors in key fields
- Student clubs and conferences
- Full-time job placement by industry and location

- Student demographics
- International and experiential learning programs
- Tuition, financial aid and scholarships
- Admissions deadlines and procedures

Now available for top schools including:
Chicago, Columbia, Harvard, Kellogg, MIT, Stanford, Tuck and Wharton

A time-saving source of comprehensive information, Clear Admit School Guides have been featured in *The Economist* and lauded by applicants, business school students and MBA graduates:

"Purchasing the Clear Admit HBS School Guide was one of best decisions I made. I visited HBS three times and have every book and pamphlet that covers the top business schools, but nothing can compare to the Clear Admit guides in offering up-to-date information on every aspect of the school's academic and social life that is not readily available on the school's website and brochures. Reading a Clear Admit School Guide gives an applicant the necessary, detailed school information to be competitive in the application process."
—An applicant to Harvard

CLEAR ADMIT
School Guides

"I want to tip my hat to the team at Clear Admit that put these guides together. I'm a recent graduate of Wharton's MBA program and remain active in the admissions process (serving as an alumni interviewer to evaluate applicants). I can't tell you how important it is for applicants to show genuine enthusiasm for Wharton and I think the Clear Admit School Guide for Wharton captures many of the important details, as well as the spirit of the school. **This sort of information is a must for the serious MBA applicant.**"
—A Wharton MBA graduate

Question #1: (e) and Question #2 (a)

www.clearadmit.com/schoolguides

contact us at mbaguides@clearadmit.com

Finally, a GMAT® prep guide series that goes beyond the basics.

Number Properties, Third Edition
ISBN: 978-0-9818533-4-5
Retail: $26

Fractions, Decimals, & Percents, Third Edition
ISBN: 978-0-9818533-2-1
Retail: $26

Equations, Inequalities, & VICs, Third Edition
ISBN: 978-0-9818533-1-4
Retail: $26

Word Translations, Third Edition
ISBN: 978-0-9818533-7-6
Retail: $26

Geometry, Third Edition
ISBN: 978-0-9818533-3-8
Retail: $26

Critical Reasoning, Third Edition
ISBN: 978-0-9818533-0-7
Retail: $26

Reading Comprehension, Third Edition
ISBN: 978-0-9818533-5-2
Retail: $26

Sentence Correction, Third Edition
ISBN: 978-0-9818533-6-9
Retail: $26

Published by

Manhattan GMAT

 You get many more pages per topic than you find in all-in-one tomes.

 Only buy those guides that address the specific skills you need to develop.

 Gain access to Online Practice GMAT Exams & Bonus Question Banks.

Now Available at your local bookstore!

COMMENTS FROM GMAT TEST TAKERS:

"Bravo, Manhattan GMAT! Bravo! The guides truly did not disappoint. All the guides are clear, concise, and well organized, and explained things in a manner that made it possible to understand things the first time through without missing any of the important details."

"I've thumbed through a lot of books that don't even touch these. The fact that they're split up into components is immeasurably helpful. The set-up of each guide and the lists of past GMAT problems make for an incredibly thorough and easy-to-follow study path."

GMAT and GMAC are registered trademarks of the Graduate Management Admission Council which neither sponsors nor endorses this product.